How Guide to Triathlons

101 Tips to Learn How to Train, Race, and Succeed in Triathlons as a Triathlete

HowExpert with Max Stoneking

Copyright HowExpert™
www.HowExpert.com

For more tips related to this topic, visit HowExpert.com/triathlons.

Recommended Resources

- HowExpert.com – How To Guides on All Topics from A to Z by Everyday Experts.
- HowExpert.com/free – Free HowExpert Email Newsletter.
- HowExpert.com/books – HowExpert Books
- HowExpert.com/courses – HowExpert Courses
- HowExpert.com/clothing – HowExpert Clothing
- HowExpert.com/membership – HowExpert Membership Site
- HowExpert.com/affiliates – HowExpert Affiliate Program
- HowExpert.com/jobs – HowExpert Jobs
- HowExpert.com/writers – Write About Your #1 Passion/Knowledge/Expertise & Become a HowExpert Author.
- HowExpert.com/resources – Additional HowExpert Recommended Resources
- YouTube.com/HowExpert – Subscribe to HowExpert YouTube.
- Instagram.com/HowExpert – Follow HowExpert on Instagram.
- Facebook.com/HowExpert – Follow HowExpert on Facebook.
- TikTok.com/@HowExpert – Follow HowExpert on TikTok.

Publisher's Foreword

Dear HowExpert Reader,

HowExpert publishes quick 'how to' guides on all topics from A to Z by everyday experts.

At HowExpert, our mission is to discover, empower, and maximize everyday people's talents to ultimately make a positive impact in the world for all topics from A to Z...one everyday expert at a time!

All of our HowExpert guides are written by everyday people just like you and me, who have a passion, knowledge, and expertise for a specific topic.

We take great pride in selecting everyday experts who have a passion, real-life experience in a topic, and excellent writing skills to teach you about the topic you are also passionate about and eager to learn.

We hope you get a lot of value from our HowExpert guides, and it can make a positive impact on your life in some way. All of our readers, including you, help us continue living our mission of positively impacting the world for all spheres of influences from A to Z.

If you enjoyed one of our HowExpert guides, then please take a moment to send us your feedback from wherever you got this book.

Thank you, and we wish you all the best in all aspects of life.

Sincerely,

BJ Min
Founder & Publisher of HowExpert
HowExpert.com

PS...If you are also interested in becoming a HowExpert author, then please visit our website at HowExpert.com/writers. Thank you & again, all the best!

COPYRIGHT, LEGAL NOTICE AND DISCLAIMER:

COPYRIGHT © BY HOT METHODS, INC. (DBA HOWEXPERT™). ALL RIGHTS RESERVED WORLDWIDE. NO PART OF THIS PUBLICATION MAY BE REPRODUCED IN ANY FORM OR BY ANY MEANS, INCLUDING SCANNING, PHOTOCOPYING, OR OTHERWISE WITHOUT PRIOR WRITTEN PERMISSION OF THE COPYRIGHT HOLDER.

DISCLAIMER AND TERMS OF USE: PLEASE NOTE THAT MUCH OF THIS PUBLICATION IS BASED ON PERSONAL EXPERIENCE AND ANECDOTAL EVIDENCE. ALTHOUGH THE AUTHOR AND PUBLISHER HAVE MADE EVERY REASONABLE ATTEMPT TO ACHIEVE COMPLETE ACCURACY OF THE CONTENT IN THIS GUIDE, THEY ASSUME NO RESPONSIBILITY FOR ERRORS OR OMISSIONS. ALSO, YOU SHOULD USE THIS INFORMATION AS YOU SEE FIT, AND AT YOUR OWN RISK. YOUR PARTICULAR SITUATION MAY NOT BE EXACTLY SUITED TO THE EXAMPLES ILLUSTRATED HERE; IN FACT, IT'S LIKELY THAT THEY WON'T BE THE SAME, AND YOU SHOULD ADJUST YOUR USE OF THE INFORMATION AND RECOMMENDATIONS ACCORDINGLY.

THE AUTHOR AND PUBLISHER DO NOT WARRANT THE PERFORMANCE, EFFECTIVENESS OR APPLICABILITY OF ANY SITES LISTED OR LINKED TO IN THIS BOOK. ALL LINKS ARE FOR INFORMATION PURPOSES ONLY AND ARE NOT WARRANTED FOR CONTENT, ACCURACY OR ANY OTHER IMPLIED OR EXPLICIT PURPOSE.

ANY TRADEMARKS, SERVICE MARKS, PRODUCT NAMES OR NAMED FEATURES ARE ASSUMED TO BE THE PROPERTY OF THEIR RESPECTIVE OWNERS, AND ARE USED ONLY FOR REFERENCE. THERE IS NO IMPLIED ENDORSEMENT IF WE USE ONE OF THESE TERMS.

NO PART OF THIS BOOK MAY BE REPRODUCED, STORED IN A RETRIEVAL SYSTEM, OR TRANSMITTED BY ANY OTHER MEANS: ELECTRONIC, MECHANICAL, PHOTOCOPYING, RECORDING, OR OTHERWISE, WITHOUT THE PRIOR WRITTEN PERMISSION OF THE AUTHOR.

ANY VIOLATION BY STEALING THIS BOOK OR DOWNLOADING OR SHARING IT ILLEGALLY WILL BE PROSECUTED BY LAWYERS TO THE FULLEST EXTENT. THIS PUBLICATION IS PROTECTED UNDER THE US COPYRIGHT ACT OF 1976 AND ALL OTHER APPLICABLE INTERNATIONAL, FEDERAL, STATE AND LOCAL LAWS AND ALL RIGHTS ARE RESERVED, INCLUDING RESALE RIGHTS: YOU ARE NOT ALLOWED TO GIVE OR SELL THIS GUIDE TO ANYONE ELSE.

THIS PUBLICATION IS DESIGNED TO PROVIDE ACCURATE AND AUTHORITATIVE INFORMATION WITH REGARD TO THE SUBJECT MATTER COVERED. IT IS SOLD WITH THE UNDERSTANDING THAT THE AUTHORS AND PUBLISHERS ARE NOT ENGAGED IN RENDERING LEGAL, FINANCIAL, OR OTHER PROFESSIONAL ADVICE. LAWS AND PRACTICES OFTEN VARY FROM STATE TO STATE AND IF LEGAL OR OTHER EXPERT ASSISTANCE IS REQUIRED, THE SERVICES OF A PROFESSIONAL SHOULD BE SOUGHT. THE AUTHORS AND PUBLISHER SPECIFICALLY DISCLAIM ANY LIABILITY THAT IS INCURRED FROM THE USE OR APPLICATION OF THE CONTENTS OF THIS BOOK.

**COPYRIGHT BY HOT METHODS, INC. (DBA HOWEXPERT™)
ALL RIGHTS RESERVED WORLDWIDE.**

Table of Contents

Recommended Resources 2
Publisher's Foreword 3
Table of Contents 5
Chapter 1: What is a Triathlon? 11
   Tip 1: Triathlon is a journey 11
   Tip 2: Inform yourself with this book! 11
   Tip 3: It's as simple as swim, bike, run 12
   Tip 4: The History 12
   Tip 5: Popular race formats 12
   Tip 6: How long does an event like this take? 13
   Tip 7: Where to sign up 13
   Tip 8: Costs 14
Chapter 2: Fun, Fit, Fast 16
   Tip 9: What it's all about 16
   Tip 10: Triathlon is special 16
   Tip 11: The health benefits 17
      At the heart 17
      Long in longevity 17
      Mental health 17
   Tip 12: The lifestyle 18
   Tip 13: The Community 18
Chapter 3: THE Gear Guide: Essentials Plus Extras 20
   Tip 14: Gear Selection 20
   Tip 15: Tech Guide 20
      The running watch 20
      The bike computer 21
      Heart rate monitor 21
      Where does my data go? 21
   Tip 16: Swim essentials 22
      Swimsuit 22
      Goggles 23
      Pool/lake/facility access 23
      Latex or silicone swimming cap 23
   Tip 17: Swim extras 23

Wetsuit	24
Pull buoy/paddles	24
Swim fins	24
Tip 18: Bike essentials	25
Getting a bike	25
Clipless pedals	25
A helmet	25
Water bottle cages	26
A reputable mechanic on hand	26
Spare tires and tubes	26
Bib or other padded shorts	26
Cycling-specific jersey	27
Tip 19: Bike extras	27
Power meter	27
Triathlon-specific/carbon bike	28
Aero helmet, aero wheels, aero cockpit	28
DIY mechanic toolset	28
Indoor trainer	28
Indoor training software	29
Tip 20: Run essentials	29
Running shoes	29
Running shirt and shorts	30
Gloves/hat/base layers for cold weather folks	30
Tip 21: Run extras	30
Multiple pairs of shoes	30
Race-specific carbon shoe	31
Treadmill access	31
Tip 22: Do I need a coach?	31
Tip 23: Miscellaneous	32
Nutritional	32
Triathlon suit	33
Recovery products	34
Chapter 4: Triad of Sports	35
Tip 24: Swimming basics	35
Comfortable in the water	35
Body position	35
"Hold" on the water	36
Breathing	36

- Open water 37
- Tip 25: Cycling basics 37
  - Get comfortable in the position 37
  - Pedaling mechanics 38
  - Get comfortable on the road 38
- Tip 26: Running basics 39
  - Mechanically limited 39
  - Run on different surfaces 39
  - Stride length and technique 39
- Tip 27: Pacing and race strategy 40
  - Pacing 40
  - Strategy 40
- Chapter 5: Training Terminology 43
  - Tip 28: By the numbers 43
  - Tip 29: Heart rate training 43
    - Alternative to swim heart rate tracking 44
  - Tip 30: What are training zones? 44
  - Tip 31: Setting zones 44
  - Tip 32: Performing tests 45
    - Swim zone test protocol 45
    - Bike zone test protocol 46
    - Run zone test protocol 46
  - Tip 33: Defining the five zones 47
    - Zone 1 training 47
    - Zone 2 training 47
    - Zone 3 training 47
    - Zone 4 training 48
    - Zone 5 training 48
  - Tip 34: Other training metrics to track 49
    - Training via pace 49
    - Training via power 50
  - Tip 35: Context is key 50
  - Tip 36: Working in your zones 50
  - Tip 37: A note on Zone 2 51
  - Tip 38: Do not compare 51
  - Tip 39: Retesting 52
- Chapter 6: The Basics of Training 54
  - Tip 40: Developing a program 54

Tip 41: Periodized and progressive 54
Tip 42: Base phase 55
Tip 43: Build phase 55
Tip 44: Race-specific phase 57
Tip 45: Taper phase 57
Tip 46: Block periodization 58
Tip 47: Applying the phases 59
Tip 48: How much of each sport to do per week? 59
Tip 49: The frequency model... 60
Tip 50: Workout types 61
    Swimming: 61
    Cycling:... 62
    Running:... 63
Tip 51: Putting it in practice with a worked example................. 64
Tip 52: Hard vs. Easy training... 68
    Hard training is stressful 68
    Hard training can be effective in small quantities 68
    What is hard? 69
    What is easy?... 69
    Easy—where the rubber meets the road 69
Tip 53: Load vs. recover... 70

Chapter 7: How to Eat 72
Tip 54: Importance of nutrition 72
Tip 55: Human metabolism—a quick overview 72
Tip 56: Eat your protein! 73
Tip 57: Food as nutrients...74
Tip 58: Fuel the training—What's the purpose? 74
    Swim nutrition 75
    Bike nutrition 75
    Run nutrition 76
Tip 59: Race Nutrition 76
Tip 60: Don't change a thing Part 1..76
Tip 61: Spare the veggies 77
Tip 62: Race morning 77
Tip 63: Don't change a thing Part 2 — the race itself.................78
Tip 64: Race hydration 78
Tip 65: Don't change a thing Part 3..79
Tip 66: During the race..79

Tip 67: Weight loss 80
Tip 68: What's the deal with carbohydrates? 81
Tip 69: Sports nutrition products 82
Tip 70: Sample nutrition plan 83
Chapter 8: How to Recover 87
Tip 71: Rest is where growth happens 87
Tip 72: Different rest periods 87
   Rest within a day 87
   Rest within a week 88
   Rest within a build-up 88
   Rest within a season 88
   Rest before the race 89
Tip 73: Understanding fatigue 89
   Acute vs. chronic 90
   What does feeling exceptional feel like? 90
   Does life permit adding more training load? 91
   Does the training data support doing more or doing less? 91
Tip 74: Sleep 91
Tip 75: Firm to bed/wake time 92
Tip 76: Capitalize on the time spent in bed 92
Tip 77: Prioritize 92
Tip 78: The "recovery workout" and active recovery 93
Tip 79: Sore or injured? 94
   Soreness 94
   Injury 94
Tip 80: Pain as a guide for injuries 94
Tip 81: Running as the injury culprit 95
Tip 82: Recovery products + tools 95
   Massage guns and massage therapy 96
   Dietary supplements 96
   Stretching and mobility 97
   Mental rest 97
Tip 83: Advanced recovery tracking 97
   Heart rate information 98
   Training software — load management 99
Chapter 9: What They Don't Tell You Before Training for and Racing in Triathlons 101
Tip 84: Know the rules of the race 101

Tip 85: Transitions 101
Tip 86: Swim to bike 102
Tip 87: Bike to run 103
   Dismount 103
   Socks? 104
   Shoes 104
   Race number 104
   Simple bike-run workflow 104
Tip 88: Setting up T1/T2 105
   Timing chip + body marking 105
   The transition spot 105
Tip 89: Aid stations 106
Tip 90: Stay for awards and post-race festivities 107
Tip 91: Open water swimming 107
Tip 92: The dreaded "bonk" 108
Tip 93: Mental strength 108
   Be positive 108
   It is a process 109
   It is not only a sport 109
Tip 94: Motivation 109
   Training with friends 110
   Sign up for a small race 110
   Switch up the music 110
   Watch the pros 111
   Embrace 111
Tip 95: Becoming a lifer 111
Tip 96: New perspectives 112
Chapter 10: The Ironman 113
Tip 97: Understand the demand of the race itself 113
Tip 98: Understand the demand for the training 113
Tip 99: Understand the demand in everyday life 114
Tip 100: Experience level 114
Tip 101: Finances 115
Chapter 11: The Ultimate Workout Index 117
About the Author 125
About the Publisher 126
Recommended Resources 127

Chapter 1: What is a Triathlon?

Tip 1: Triathlon is a journey

"Success is a journey, not an outcome. The doing is often more important than the outcome." —Arthur Ashe

A journey worth taking is that of preparing for a triathlon. The sport is funky—three sports in one! The sport is demanding. Most importantly, the sport is representative of what can happen when commitment and determination collide. Race day itself is a polished summary of the sacrifice, the planning, and the discipline that comprised the months or years leading into the event.

It would be all well and good if one could become a triathlete by following a few simple steps, but that is not how the sport operates. Treating the process like a journey is not so much an ethos as it is a necessity. To master swimming, biking, and running, sometimes over extreme distances, the athlete must have a long-term approach to making key physical and mental adaptations that will develop the ability to endure the challenge.

Get comfortable with being referred to as "the athlete." That is what you are now.

Tip 2: Inform yourself with this book!

If a few simple steps cannot summarize, then 101+ should do. This handbook serves as an immersive guide for how to develop the athletic acumen necessary to cross the finish line at your next event. Topics covered include investment in proper gear, structuring your training, managing non-training life, and more. There is something for all disciplines in the sport, for all distances, and for all ability levels. Whether you are aiming to complete your first race or need guidance after years in the sport, this guide is THE resource to train, compete, and succeed in the sport of triathlon.

Tip 3: It's as simple as swim, bike, run

In that order. Always.

Okay, there are some exceptions. And simple? There is a lot to unpack!

Tip 4: The History

The sport of triathlon burst on the sporting scene in 1974 in San Diego, California, with the first-ever advertised swim/bike/run event, yet to be called triathlon formally. In 1978, an ultra-distance form of the sport was born with what was known as the "Hawaii Ironman." This event consisted of a 2.4-mile swim, a 112-mile bike, and a 26.2-mile marathon run. This distance format still exists today and is known as the Ironman. There are now many Ironman distance races held globally.

The Ironman distance is not the only format in the sport of triathlon. Since its inception, the formats for race distances and events have expanded widely. The Olympic distance, for example, is another format that is popular worldwide and follows the format that is competed in at the Olympic games. Triathlon first became an Olympic sport in the 2000 Sydney Olympic games.

At its core, the triathlon is a swim, a bike, and a run, all done in succession and split up by a transition between each. The goal is to make this transition as efficient as possible because it does count into the overall time.

Tip 5: Popular race formats

The most common races an athlete may find when looking for an event are:

Event	Swim	Bike	Run
Sprint distance	400 meters	12.5 miles/20km	3.1 miles/5km
Olympic distance	1500 meters (~1mile)	25 miles/40km	6.2 miles/10km
Half Ironman	1.2 miles/1900m	56 miles/90km	13.1 miles/21km
Ironman	2.4 miles/3800m	112 miles/180km	26.2 miles/42km

Some race organizers create their own distance or involve an off-roading element like the popular XTERRA series, where the biking is done on a mountain bike, and the run is on a rocky trail. Other events involve multiple bouts of mini triathlons that are not necessarily in the standard order, known as the Triple Mix format. This is a testament to the vastness of the options for triathlon beyond that of the standard distances. Each distance requires a unique set of skills, whether it be speed or extreme endurance, to name a few.

Tip 6: How long does an event like this take?

Event duration varies greatly depending on the distance chosen and the athlete's ability level. For example, an elite-level sprint distance athlete will regularly turn in times under an hour, while a first-time Ironman athlete may be on the course for over 15 hours.

The important piece to remember is to understand the demands of the race. The last thing any athlete wants is to be on the course for hours longer than anticipated. Through a periodized and progressed training program, the athlete can develop a general sense of how long each discipline may take for a given distance. If the race is long enough, it may warrant developing a nutrition plan, a topic outlined in detail in **Chapter 7**.

Tip 7: Where to sign up

A quick Google search can often point an athlete in the right direction. Active.com is a resource that houses many of the popular race registrations and includes a location function so that local races pop up if desired. Triathlon is a sport that can take an athlete around the globe, and many athletes turn race opportunities into destination races in some of the most popular beach or mountain locales.

When signing up, an athlete will choose the age group he or she belongs to, and that age group will be used to assign awards at the end of a race. There is often an overall awards category and then specific age award categories, e.g., males 40-44.

Signing up early is encouraged. Some races limit the number of participants. Furthermore, early sign-up can sometimes be rewarded in the form of a discount on race entry.

Tip 8: Costs

Triathlon is a pricey sport. This book would be remiss not to address that upfront. Most of the costs incurred are associated with training and gear, which will be discussed in **Chapter 3**. Still, races themselves can be expensive, especially if the athlete chooses to travel by air and spend multiple nights in a hotel.

The average cost for a sprint or Olympic distance race generally is around $100, but Ironman distance races can exceed $500.

It is important for the athlete to take race entry fees and travel costs into account when planning a race weekend or a full season. Season planning is covered further in **Chapter 6**.

Chapter Review

This chapter covered the following:

- How triathlon is more than an event; it's a journey
- How triathlon came to be

- How to understand race distances
- How to plan for sign-up and race fees

Equipped with a basic understanding of what a triathlon is, you are now ready to tackle training. Before the training talk begins, however, deepening your understanding of how triathlon is greater than "one big day" is needed to appreciate the journey.

Chapter 2: Fun, Fit, Fast

Tip 9: What it's all about

Take notice of how "fun" is placed before fit and fast. It is true that to have a life-best, fast performance, the athlete must be fit, but not every triathlete is in the sport for the fast. As an amateur, you are not your performance. You likely do not make a living from triathlon. If you are an athlete contemplating whether to do a triathlon, making the journey fun is an essential first step to setting up a successful training plan.

Tip 10: Triathlon is special

Outcomes such as forging relationships, finding mentors, or improving confidence have little to no connection with the position in which the athlete crosses the finish line. Success need not always be measured in competitive performance. Every athlete comes into a race with a reason to be there. One athlete may be on a 100+ lb. weight loss journey, while another may be able to maintain positive mental health from training and racing. Of course, if the athlete is in the market for maximizing athletic potential, triathlon is prime for that as well.

Regardless, triathlon has its way of developing attributes that are associated with common definitions of success, whether that be confidence, health, or accountability, among many others. These are traits of high performers, and the nature of taking on the challenge of a triathlon is enough to take an athlete from a layperson to a high performer. The requisite training and commitment, especially in the longer distances, is a transformative experience. Triathlon is special in this way.

Tip 11: *The health benefits*

Exercise is a proven tool to enhance well-being and increase longevity. Triathlon is the antidote for anyone looking to upgrade his or her health package. It is impossible to do a triathlon without exercising.

At the heart

The central component of triathlon is cardiovascular fitness, and to keep it short, an athlete on a proper training program will achieve far higher than average cardiovascular fitness markers. There is something critical about human movement that creates a cascade of positive health effects, including blood pressure regulation, bone and tendon health, blood vessel function, and immune health.

Long in longevity

Triathlon may not be a guaranteed gateway to perfect health, but the structure and modality in which it is delivered provide a framework to boost longevity. A sustainable training program is one that many triathletes find being able to roll for many years. There is a reason races have 70+ age categories! They know how to go long!

Mental health

Some of the training required for long-distance triathlon races like Ironman develop an immense ability to endure on a physical level, but also on a mental level. For example, hours 10, 11, and 12 in an Ironman are hardly a feat of physical fitness. However, mental fortitude brings the athlete through the marathon and across the finish line.

This is not to say that everyone needs to do an Ironman. An athlete may only be at the level where training and racing a sprint triathlon is a challenge. The same theme persists. Habitually conquering challenging training sessions can improve the athlete's self-confidence and mindset for taking on other daunting tasks in the workplace or in family life.

As mentioned earlier, training is not the be-all and end-all of the sport, although it is easy to get lost in one's performance condition. Fun is the priority, and the athlete having the most fun should be a happy athlete. A sense of reason and purpose to keep showing up each day is a reason to be happy and is positive for mental health.

Tip 12: The lifestyle

Many Type A personalities flock to the sport of triathlon because it is another high-level activity to add to their Rolodex. Type A people enjoy being competitive and structuring a schedule in a way that allows becoming better at being competitive. To take performance to a high level, an athlete must find joy in the competitive spirit and hold true to a training program for many months. So, while triathlon may attract Type A's, there is also reason to believe it produces them as well.

It is important for the athlete to remember that the triathlon lifestyle does not mean that triathlon must consume one's life. Amateurs often have family and work-life obligations to prioritize, and many have been successful in working a training plan around those elements. If you have a love for exercise and competing and can stick to a plan, you can embody the lifestyle.

Tip 13: The Community

Perhaps the best has been saved for last. The triathlon community has a certain vibe to it that can be motivating for an athlete. Groups often assemble for running workouts, bike rides, or a swim squad to keep the training from becoming monotonous. The community also offers support on race day. There is nothing more invigorating than hearing a volunteer shout some encouraging words when feeling smashed in the final miles of the run. The volunteers, the athletes, and the mentors all make up a tight-knit group that is the world of triathlon.

The athlete competes as an individual on race day, but there is almost always a team of supporters or mentors behind each performance. Triathlon is too hard to go at it alone. The camaraderie keeps the sport fun, and after all, fun is what it's all about.

Chapter Review

This chapter covered the following:

- What triathlon is all about
- How triathlon is a special sport
- The health benefits associated with the sport, physical and mental
- What it means to embody the "triathlon lifestyle"
- The impact of the community within the sport

It is clear now that triathlon is greater than "one big day." Training, developing as an athlete, and connecting with the community along the way toward an event is a transformative experience.

To have this experience, the athlete needs to acquire some baseline equipment to train and compete at a level that fosters success. Chapter 3 is the athlete's guide to investing in gear.

Chapter 3: THE Gear Guide: Essentials Plus Extras

Tip 14: Gear Selection

One of the pitfalls of triathlon is that proper gear is not only necessary but also expensive. The options for gear are endless. It is easy to go down the rabbit hole to justify the purchase of the next best gadget.

At the bare minimum, an athlete needs to have a working bike, a pair of running shoes, swimming goggles, and a swimsuit. However, an athlete can enhance the training and racing experience by investing money into quality gear that will last through the day-to-day training and multiple races. Therefore, the remainder of the chapter will cover the essential and discretionary items for each discipline in the triathlon.

Tip 15: Tech Guide

Wearable technology has become a staple item in the endurance sports space. Companies like Garmin, Wahoo, and Polar have made acquiring training data a simple process for any athlete. Given that data is an important piece of any training program, covered at length in **Chapter 4,** investing in some type of wearable is recommended.

The running watch

Many options exist on the running watch market. The most basic watches can use GPS to track pace and distance, and this need not be limited to only running. For example, a budget-friendly way to train for a triathlon is to purchase a reliable watch and use it to track swimming, cycling, and running training. Consider it the hub from which all of the training data is gathered.

Most watches by Garmin, Wahoo, or Polar also offer a wrist-based heart rate monitor, but the most accurate heart rate data is acquired with a chest strap that syncs to the watch.

The bike computer

A particularly savvy piece of equipment is a bike computer. Most computers are equipped with GPS functions and the ability to connect other sensors such as a power meter, heart rate, cell phone, and other devices. The computer is usually attached to a mount fastened to the bike, and the display includes data screens showing metrics such as average speed, power output, and heart rate. Most models also feature a map that can be helpful for navigation while riding. Some of the higher-end models have functions that go far beyond what a beginner triathlete would ever need, making the bike computer not an essential piece of technology. In fact, the newer running watches are enabled with similar functions for displaying power, heart rate, and other metrics. An athlete can get a great start with a quality running watch.

Heart rate monitor

As mentioned, the most accurate way to collect heart rate data is through a chest strap. These are typically inexpensive items, given how long they last. A quality product from Garmin may cost an athlete around $100, but other brands offer a similar technology for cheaper. **Chapters 5 and 6** speak to the importance of heart rate training, and a heart rate chest strap is a high-priority item for athletes looking to be serious about training.

Where does my data go?

A platform to house training data can be as simple as using a journal or as complex as purchasing some available software. At a minimum, an athlete should be aware of how the workouts have gone to spot trends that show improvement or lack thereof. This is how coaches or self-coached athletes can make necessary adjustments to a plan.

Companies such as Garmin, Wahoo, and Polar each have apps that connect seamlessly to a running watch or bike computer. These apps have basic functions such as tracking training distance, pace, and heart rate and organizing it into a useful summary for the athlete. For most novice athletes, this is an efficient way to start with tracking.

Another popular app is TrainingPeaks which is more detailed than the apps native to Garmin, Wahoo, and Polar. With TrainingPeaks, the data from a watch or computer is uploaded to the platform and can be analyzed on a deeper level than in other apps. With the analysis, an athlete can form a digital training journal. The platform is also useful for creating a training calendar, and many coaches can communicate with athletes through the app when scheduling a week or month of training. There is a monthly membership option for $19.95 or a yearly option for $119 to gain access to all the features. TrainingPeaks is highly recommended, but not required, for an athlete looking to remain in the sport for multiple seasons.

More in line with social media, Strava is an app that allows an athlete to connect with other users to share training activities in a news feed. While there are useful features for tracking training data, the app is commonly used for social features. Seeing how friends or competitors are training keeps the process fun and is preferred by some. There is also a live leaderboard for segments out on the roads or trails. Users create the segments using GPS data, and then the community can battle it out to take the top spot, known as a KOM (King of the Mountain) or QOM (Queen of the Mountain). Gamification of training has been one of the most popular motivators in the last 5-10 years.

Tip 16: Swim essentials

Swimming can be a sport where it is easy to get carried away with nonessential gear. However, the basics will usually be sufficient and can free up money in the budget for other gear.

<u>Swimsuit</u>

A quality swimsuit is a must. Being comfortable in the water is an important part of making swim training effective, and competitive swimwear is a sure bet to feeling more comfortable. It is also worth noting that many novice athletes are new to swimming, and a normal pair of shorts, or shorts plus top, induce drag, making buoyancy much more difficult.

Goggles

Swimming without goggles is not recommended. A durable pair usually is inexpensive and will last a season or two. Speedo, TYR, and Arena are some well-known brands to be on the lookout for.

Pool/lake/facility access

To practice swimming, the athlete needs to have access to water. Warmer climate locales may have public swimming beaches that can be a great option for an athlete not looking to spend money on a pool membership. However, for most training programs, it is recommended to have access to an indoor or outdoor swimming pool to make the most of the swim training. The cost of a pool membership is variable depending on the facility.

Latex or silicone swimming cap

While not absolutely essential, a latex or silicone swimming cap can be helpful for maintaining the integrity of hair and keeping water out of the ears. If an athlete has long hair, the cap can also keep hair out of the eyes while swimming. Given that most races require a swimming cap to be worn, it is best practice to train with a cap so as not to be unfamiliar come race day. Caps are typically inexpensive, and having a few on hand can be useful as they are subject to breakage.

Tip 17: Swim extras

The extras are highly recommended for an athlete who can dedicate a significant chunk of time each week to improving swimming.

Wetsuit

Many races feature a lake swim that takes place in cold water. A wetsuit provides insulation during the swim and buoyancy to the athlete. Depending on the race, the wetsuit may be required or disallowed. This is dependent on what the race organizers deem cold water or warm water. Most triathlons outlaw wetsuits at water warmer than 78 degrees. Warmer water increases an athlete's chance of overheating, which is why the rules are in place.

If targeting a race that takes place in the spring or in the fall where water temps can be below 70 degrees, factoring a wetsuit rental or purchase into the budget is recommended to ensure a smooth race experience.

Pull buoy/paddles

Building swim-specific arm strength is a way for a novice swimmer to take his or her swimming to a higher level. Longer distance races inherently have longer swims, and it is crucial to finish the swim with plenty of energy for a bike and run.

Using a pull buoy and paddles during swim training is a common way to instruct the swimmer into maintaining body position and catching the water properly. The paddles reinforce the catch while the buoy affords added buoyancy. However, paddles and buoys are not allowed during races.

Swim fins

Learning how to use legs to kick in swimming is a skill that confuses many first-time triathletes. Kicking is required to maintain body position, and if not trained to do so can result in more effort than required being put into the swim. Swim fins enforce proper kick mechanics and can be a tool used during normal swim training. However, fins are not allowed during races.

Tip 18: Bike essentials

If swimming was easy to get carried away with gear selection, cycling just blew that out of the water. A bicycle has many working parts, and there are endless options for upgrading said parts. The apparel scene in cycling is also vast but often includes gear that the average athlete will not need.

Getting a bike

This should go without saying. To do a triathlon, an athlete needs a working bicycle. However, the type of bike is not all that important for a novice. If an athlete is looking to finish, a simple hybrid or mountain bike will be plenty. However, if the athlete is targeting a longer distance or going for performance, a road bike is highly recommended, and a triathlon-specific bike is even better (covered more in **Tip 19**). A great resource for buying a used bike is Facebook Marketplace, but an athlete can opt to purchase a brand-new bike. The price range on bikes is wide, but a reliable and standard bike can be found for less than $500 in most cases.

Clipless pedals

Clipless pedals are somewhat of a misnomer. These pedals actually involve clipping shoes into the pedals. Any serious triathlete will want to invest in these as well as cycling cleats, as the pedaling efficiency and overall comfort on the bike are greatly improved. Not only can power be applied on the push phase of the pedal stroke, but when clipped in, the athlete can pull up on the pedal, too, to gain more momentum. There is a learning curve associated with clipping in and out to start and stop riding, but most athletes master this skill quickly and immediately see the advantages over flat pedals and tennis shoes.

A helmet

Helmets are required at all races for safety reasons, and a helmet should always be worn during outdoor training rides. Riding a bike can be dangerous, and motorists are not always aware of how to share the road with a cyclist.

Water bottle cages

Hydration is an important aspect of both training and racing on the bike. In any race longer than a sprint distance, an athlete will need to have adequate hydration, and water bottle cages can solve this issue. During training, many rides will be longer than an hour, and the same principles of hydration apply. Bikes can be fitted with one, two, or sometimes multiple cages. The standard is two, but this is up to the athlete to decide. Cages are typically inexpensive and can be installed with ease.

A reputable mechanic on hand

Keeping a bike in working order is essential. The last thing an athlete wants is not to be able to rely on the bike when he or she is pushing to the limit during a race or in a training session. Becoming familiar with a local bike shop is a great way to maintain a bike and develop a resource in the event of a mechanical issue. Some bike shops offer courses on how to perform DIY maintenance on a bike. This would include tasks such as changing a flat tire or replacing a broken chain. The more an athlete takes ownership of his or her equipment, the better off the overall cycling experience can be.

Spare tires and tubes

Tires go flat. That is part of the cost of doing business when riding a bike. Fortunately, a spare inner tube (the part that inflates) is usually all an athlete will need to get back on the road. Rarely does the full tire blow out. Installing a new tube is simple after a few practice trials and is a valuable skill to learn. Having a spare is also valuable if a tire goes flat during a race. Changing the tire quickly can save seconds or minutes in the overall race time. Athletes typically have a spare kit attached to the bike for training and racing.

Bib or other padded shorts

Given that most training programs involve multiple months of consistent riding, it is crucial that the athlete is comfortable on the bike. Three points of contact exist between the rider and the bike; arguably, the most important point is between the legs. A padded pair of shorts or bib shorts feature some cushion without becoming too bunched. The cushion increases comfort and can extend the amount of time an athlete can spend on the bike. In addition, the bib-type shorts help keep the cushion in place, so there is no chaffing in the area.

Cycling-specific jersey

An athlete looking to race a sprint distance race may not be training at a volume necessary for a cycling jersey, but for higher volume athletes, a cycling jersey is a must. Jerseys feature pockets in the back that can hold a phone, keys, wallet, and nutrition, amongst other important items. It is important to have these items on hand, and the cycling jersey concept is the solution.

Jerseys also are made of breathable fabric and can wick away sweat. This keeps the athlete cool during training sessions.

Tip 19: Bike extras

The extras are highly recommended for an athlete who can put in the training time necessary to reap the benefits of such upgrades. It is easy to "buy speed" in the cycling world, but most of the extras to be discussed below are worthy investments for improving fitness or improving the bike ownership experience of the athlete.

Power meter

Power meters measure the amount of strain an athlete puts through the drivetrain or pedal of the bike to reflect a measure of output in watts. Entire training programs can be set up based on cycling power; thus, the power meter is a useful tool for training. However, most power meters cost more than $400, and an athlete must be certain that the sport of triathlon is a long-term commitment to make this item worth the expense.

Triathlon-specific/carbon bike

Triathlon bikes are faster. There is no way around that statement, and most serious triathletes spend the money on a triathlon bike because no matter the race distance, the most time can be made up during the bike portion. In addition, the "tri bike" offers a signature aero position that puts an athlete's hands out in front in a tucked position to minimize drag and increase efficiency. The biggest aerodynamic penalty on a bike is the rider; thus, getting into an aero position is a simple way to minimize drag.

Aero helmet, aero wheels, aero cockpit

Aero add-ons are what define "buying speed." Any type of lighter or more aerodynamic upgrade to a bike is intended to make the athlete faster on the bike for the same or less effort than if he or she did not have these items. It is recommended to place emphasis on building the fitness necessary to complete the race distance before worrying about shelling out hundreds of dollars on aero equipment. They provide marginal gains in most cases.

DIY mechanic toolset

Purchasing a basic toolset for bike maintenance is a great investment to capitalize on the mechanical skills courses discussed previously. If the athlete has a firm understanding of working on a bike, acquiring the tools can help avoid hefty labor costs from local bike shops. Bikes can be complex, which is why this is an optional item. Besides, supporting the local bike shop is always a great idea!

Indoor trainer

An athlete looking to train year-round or during winter months will benefit from having an indoor trainer. The most basic trainers involve attaching the bike to the unit and pedaling against the resistance. This is referred to as a "dumb" trainer or "fluid" trainer.

A higher-level product is that of a smart trainer, which may include a wheel-on setup or a direct drive setup.

In a wheel-on trainer, the setup is identical to the "dumb" trainer, but the resistance can be varied during the ride via Bluetooth connection to simulate sensations similar to outdoor riding. A typical wheel-on smart trainer costs $300-500, depending on the brand. Saris, TacX, and Wahoo make up the bulk of the market share for these devices.

A direct drive trainer involves removing the bike's rear wheel and attaching it to a unit that acts as a large, controlled flywheel. Bluetooth connection varies the resistance to simulate outdoor sensations. The sensation is far more realistic than the wheel-on variety, and most direct-drive devices are equipped with a power meter. A typical direct drive smart trainer costs $600-1,100, depending on the brand. Saris, TacX, and Wahoo make up the bulk of the market share for these devices.

Indoor training software

Apps have been created to run on computers or tablets that simulate outdoor riding to make the indoor riding experience more interactive. The smart trainer connects to the apps via Bluetooth. The two most popular are Zwift and TrainerRoad. Specific workouts and entire training plans can be found within the two platforms. Zwift is priced at $15 per month, while TrainerRoad is priced at $20 per month. Both offer a free trial period.

Tip 20: Run essentials

Running is a relatively minimalist sport. A pair of shoes fit for running, and an athlete is ready to go. However, some more detailed items should be regarded as essential to keep the athlete comfortable during training.

Running shoes

It is advised that the shoes an athlete chooses for running are both comfortable and made for running. Logging hundreds of miles on a pair of flimsy shoes is a recipe for injury. Major brands such as Nike, Adidas, Brooks, New Balance, Saucony, Asics, and others make a wide range of shoes at a wide range of price points. There is something for everyone, and a quality pair of running shoes can go a long way.

Running shirt and shorts

Many triathlons take place during the summer months, which means that the training also occurs during those months. Running in hot weather is already uncomfortable, and improper clothing in hot weather is undesirable. A lightweight pair of running shorts and a running tank top or shirt can keep an athlete cool so the training gets done no matter the weather.

Gloves/hat/base layers for cold weather folks

Running in the heat is hard, but so is running in the cold. A winter run without proper layers can turn ugly in a hurry. If the athlete must train in a climate where the weather is below freezing, a standard apparel lineup should include:

- Lightweight gloves
- Leggings
- A zip-up jacket for wind protection
- A beanie or winter hat

Those four items should be plenty to get an athlete through a winter of running.

Tip 21: Run extras

Sticking with the minimalist theme, the extras for running are rather sparse. There is not a laundry list of nonessential or essential items like in cycling or swimming.

Multiple pairs of shoes

A common practice amongst runners and triathletes is having a shoe rotation of 2-5 different shoes. This is because athletes need rest days and so do the shoes. Seriously. The foam in the shoes requires 24-48 hours of rebound time due to the compression placed on them during a run. Furthermore, running in a few different types of shoes challenges foot mechanics slightly and can help build the foot strength needed to prevent injury.

Athletes may also prefer to have a cushioned shoe for easy running, a standard shoe for longer running, and a firm shoe for fast workouts.

Race-specific carbon shoe

All the hype in the endurance sports community as of late has been around the advent of the "super shoe." This type of shoe was pioneered by Nike and features a carbon sole that is intended to improve the efficiency of the runner, thus making them work less for the same effort. Other brands have since adopted similar technology. There is no doubt that the technology of the carbon sole works, as evidenced by numerous running records having been shattered since the onset of the shoes circa 2013. Unfortunately, most "super shoes" run in the $170-$250 range and do not last as long as a normal, everyday running shoe. An athlete must keep this in mind when developing a triathlon gear budget.

Treadmill access

The treadmill can be a great running tool for a variety of reasons. For example, many athletes use treadmills during rainy or snowy weather to avoid the elements. Other athletes welcome a soft surface and controlled environment during running. However, it is not essential to have access to a treadmill for triathlon training, and usually, it will require a gym membership in some capacity.

Tip 22: Do I need a coach?

That is an important question. Many athletes would not dare prepare for a triathlon without consulting a coach, while others feel comfortable developing a training program by themselves. A coach can provide a few important items:

- Basic or detailed framework for training
- Objective feedback on how the program is going
- Motivation to keep going when training or life becomes hectic
- A voice of reason when the plan or program needs to change
- Years of experience both competing and helping other athletes become successful in triathlon
- Tips for race strategy for a variety of distances
- Insight into the athlete's strengths and limiters

It should be noted that while each one of those elements above is helpful for succeeding in the sport, a coach does not typically work for free. If the athlete is on a limited budget or just starting his or her triathlon foray, it may be useful to spend money on a self-coached training program or on equipment that will allow the training to get done. Remember, entering a race costs money too!

Nonetheless, the return on investment of having a coach is high, and an athlete looking to seriously invest in triathlon needs to regard employing a coach as a priority.

Tip 23: Miscellaneous

There are some items not specific to a particular discipline that an athlete would benefit from having on hand. Some items are essential, and others would be best off being purchased after an athlete has mastered the basics or decided to commit to triathlon long-term.

Nutritional

Nutrition is often regarded as the 4th discipline in triathlon. The longer the distance, the more important nutrition becomes. **Chapter 7** covers the topic in-depth, but an overview of essential nutrition items is worth reviewing.

Lumped in with nutrition is hydration, and an athlete can benefit from having an electrolyte powder, tablet, or beverage available during most training sessions. Easy sessions that take less than an hour usually only warrant plain water. However, when an athlete may be stacking multiple workouts together in a single day or when the weather is particularly hot, there is a need for an electrolyte supplement. Staying hydrated can make or break a workout, accelerate recovery, and prevent cramping during race situations.

NUUN sport and Science in Sport are two brands that make sugar-free tablets in a variety of flavors that can be dropped into water. Drinks such as Gatorade and Powerade are acceptable but do contain a significant amount of sugar. The purpose of sugar in endurance sports should not be understated, but there is some nuance when it comes to mixing sugar and electrolytes. Sugar is not always needed when electrolytes are needed. This is discussed further in **Chapter 7.**

To reap the benefits of proper hydration, an athlete needs a bottle(s) to put the liquid in. A high-quality set of water bottles can go a long way in triathlon; for training, a bottle that can hold 28-32 oz or 850-1,000 mL is a good shout. For a race, specifically on a bike, the bottles can be a bit smaller to be less of a weight penalty.

An athlete would also benefit from finding a reliable sports nutrition product in the form of gels, powdered drink mix, or chews. Reliable, in this case, means that the product does not upset the stomach or cause other digestive issues. **Chapter 7** explains the importance of sports nutrition products and when to use them over real food.

Triathlon suit

A jack-of-all-trades item is the triathlon suit. It is not essential for an athlete to own one, but it can make a longer distance race experience more enjoyable from a comfort standpoint. A standard suit comes in a sleeveless or a sleeved version and covers all of the torso and the legs down to the knee. Most suits are skin-tight and can be worn in the water during the swim portion. They also feature a small area of padding, like cycling shorts, to make the bike portion more comfortable. This padding is strategically smaller than a normal bike short to allow for comfortable running and minimal chafing. Brands such as Zoot, ROKA, 2XU, and others make a range of suits priced from $100 to $500. If an athlete is not looking to spend money on a triathlon suit, some brands offer special triathlon shorts to be worn throughout swim, bike, and run. In a short race, a normal swimsuit can often be enough to maintain comfort and ease the transition from one discipline to the next.

Recovery products

If an athlete is controlling training intensity, eating/hydrating right, and sleeping enough, then there is often no need to shell out money on recovery products if the budget does not allow it. Recovery products include a foam roller, a massage gun, special supplements, and Kinesio tape. This does not mean that these items are not effective, but the big-ticket items to recovering properly are proper training, proper eating, and proper sleeping. After an athlete has mastered these basics, can he or she begin to invest in products that will provide marginal gains, if any? Unfortunately, many passive modalities like massage guns or Kinesio tape are sparsely supported by the literature in terms of efficacy. When in doubt, leave it out regarding a product that is advertised as "boosting recovery."

Chapter Review

This chapter covered the following:

- A detailed guide to training technology
- Essential and extra gear for swimming
- Essential and extra gear for cycling
- Essential and extra gear for running
- Answering the question, "Do I need a coach?"
- Important miscellaneous items an athlete may want to purchase

Once the athlete has the budget set for gear, it's time to learn about basic technical skills. **Chapter 4** goes in-depth on the technique behind swim, bike, and run.

Chapter 4: Triad of Sports

Basic technical skills can go a long way in a triathlon. An athlete with a sound technical base in swimming, biking, and running will be able to maximize performance and get across the finish line feeling accomplished.

Tip 24: *Swimming basics*

Swimming may be the most difficult discipline of the three sports. Many new triathletes do not have a swimming background or have never swum before, and the water behaves differently than sports done on land. Putting more physical effort into the bike or the run usually results in going faster. In swimming, more effort can result in technical breakdown and going *slower*. Fast with minimal effort is the name of the game in triathlon swimming. Typically, an athlete cannot win the race in the swim, but he or she certainly can make the bike and run far easier by mastering basic swimming skills. The swimming section of this chapter covers the basics. It is more in-depth than the guidance for learning to run or ride a bike, as technique is less of the overall contribution to success in those sports.

Comfortable in the water

Becoming comfortable in the water is a priority when starting a swim training program. If the athlete is looking to compete in a triathlon and is fearful of the water, working with a certified swim instructor for swim lessons is recommended. In addition, basic water skills such as floating and treading water are potential building blocks to becoming a swimmer.

Body position

If the athlete has some water experience or is gung-ho about being in the water, beginning to work on body position is paramount. The more on top of the water an athlete can be, the more efficient swimming can be. Head, hips, and feet must all be in a line to achieve good body position.

- **Head:** Should be pointed down and only needs to move to take a breath
- **Hips:** Should remain at the surface and in line with the shoulders. Fishtailing down the pool is a sign of insufficient kick or pulling strength
- **Feet:** The athlete must kick to keep the feet at the surface. Kicking in triathlon swimming is not so much for propulsion as it is for *balance.*

It is common for hips to sink in the water either from a lack of upper body strength to pull through the water or from a lack of understanding how to kick. The pull buoy mentioned in **Chapter 3** is a fantastic item to force the athlete's hips to the surface. It is usually a foam buoy that goes between the legs and aids in floatation. As the athlete becomes more aware of body *balance*, usually gained through repetition or working with a coach, the pull buoy can be tapered off so that the athlete reinforces swimming without assistance.

"Hold" on the water

Pulling the water is a major part of swimming. The common term in the swimming community is having a good "hold" on the water. It may seem counterintuitive, but the water can act as a platform to leverage the body. When the athlete has leverage, the pull becomes propulsive. This requires using the entire arm to power through the water.

It is common for novice swimmers to swim like a T-rex, only pulling from the elbow to the hand. However, the entire arm is fair game for pulling and will result in larger muscles being used. Larger muscles do not fatigue as quickly. Developing swim-specific upper body strength takes time and is best achieved when the athlete commits to making it to the pool 2-3 times per week.

Breathing

Swimming requires holding one's breath. There is no way around it. Breath holding can be a tricky skill to master, especially when swimming can make an athlete out of breath. One of the major contributors to athletes struggling with breathing is not timing the breath correctly. When mistimed, the athlete may become panicked, leading to a sense of overexertion. One way to combat this is using a set breathing pattern because it takes the thinking out of when the athlete needs to breathe. Every third stroke is a great place to start. Think, "One, Two, Breathe!".

Not only does the breathing pattern afford a structure to relax and breathe, but it also encourages better body position. Using a bilateral technique like every 3, the athlete will have to breathe to both sides. When breathing to both sides, there is an equal rotation of the hips and torso in both directions leading to improved efficiency. "Bilateral three-stroke" is not the only pattern available, but for a novice swimmer, it can take the hassle out of understanding the concept of breathing in swimming.

Open water

Practicing swimming in a pool is ideal for standardizing training, but an open-water swim is what is most common in triathlon races. A lake or ocean swim can be quite different from pool swimming in that the water is murky, the athlete must sight for buoys, there may be hundreds of other people swimming, and there may be swells of waves. It is highly recommended that the athlete tries swimming in open water at least once before an event to ensure comfort on race day. This may best be accomplished by seeking out a local swim group to practice safely and comfortably.

Tip 25: Cycling basics

It should go without saying that an athlete must know how to ride a bike to compete in a triathlon. Other than knowing how, the basics of cycling are quite simple. Put more pressure into the pedals, and the faster one will go. Some pointers in terms of pedaling and handling on the roads can be helpful.

Get comfortable in the position

If an athlete has purchased a road bike or triathlon-specific bike, the sitting position on the bike can be uncomfortable at first. These bikes are designed for speed rather than comfort, but it does not mean a comfortable position cannot be found on these bikes. Most comfort comes from riding often. Over time, muscles and tendons adapt to the position to become more comfortable.

If there is a particular area of discomfort at the feet, between the legs, or in the upper body, it can be worth adjusting parts of the bike to be more comfortable. Some common areas to adjust are handlebars, seat height, and seat type. Most first-time triathletes would benefit from being comfortable before being fast.

Pedaling mechanics

Clipless pedals are a highly recommended purchase for a triathlete because when clipped in, an athlete can pull up and push down during the pedal stroke. A foot strap option is also available for those opting to wear only tennis shoes on the bike. Either way, pedaling efficiency, and power production can be improved when the foot is in a fixed position.

Pedaling cadence, or revolutions of the cranks per minute, is another important technical aspect. An athlete will want to refrain from grinding along at a low cadence because it can be quite taxing on the muscles. Similarly, a high cadence can also inhibit the amount of power produced because the athlete is "spinning" the gears. A comfortable cadence can be found through experience, and usually, an athlete will self-select a natural pedal stroke after a few rides. The use of shifting gears on the bike can be helpful in maintaining a cadence that keeps even pressure on the pedals throughout a race or ride.

Get comfortable on the road

The open road can be a hectic place for a cyclist. Motorists, weather, and other cyclists are a few items to be aware of when riding on the road. It is recommended that an athlete spends time training on the road to practice this awareness. Being on the road also forces the practice of braking, turning, going uphill, and going downhill. Experiencing different speeds in training will help with comfort in a race when the effort is high.

Tip 26: Running basics

Mechanically limited

Due to the high-impact nature of running, there is a limitation on the amount of running that can be placed in a training program. This is especially true for a novice athlete who is new to running. On the other hand, cycling and swimming have a low impact, and if the cardiovascular system is good, it could be done indefinitely.

One strategy to complete a run training program injury free is to increase both mileage and intensity slowly. For example, an athlete who has never run before may engage in a run/walk program before beginning to run to build a tolerance to ground forces. Furthermore, running at a high intensity places more load on the legs than when running easy. This is another reason why intensity and mileage should be increased slowly and never should be increased at the same time.

Run on different surfaces

If an athlete is having a hard time adjusting to running over concrete or asphalt for daily training, switching up the surface can be helpful. For example, finding a soft dirt trail at a park or gaining access to a treadmill can be a way to run on a more forgiving surface. Footwear, mentioned in **Chapter 3**, can also improve comfort while running, and many options exist to find the most comfortable fit.

Stride length and technique

Most of the time, the athlete's natural running stride will be the most efficient because it is the most familiar and comfortable. However, some basic pointers to improving run efficiency do exist to help the athlete relax:

- Stand tall, shoulders relaxed, chest forward, head up
- Slight forward lean

- Hands relaxed and thumbs up
- Quick feet

Having a relaxed upper body decreases the tension that can often prevent an athlete from feeling relaxed when running. In addition, quick feet and a high cadence are preferred in running to reduce the forces of impact.

Tip 27: Pacing and race strategy

Pacing

Pacing is a technical skill that requires practice and can make or break a race performance. Starting out too hard in a race can put an athlete beyond his or her physical limits. While a race is a great time to push those limits, the best race is the one that is executed well over the course of swimming, biking, and running.

The easiest way to pace any race is to avoid operating at intensity or effort that was never a part of the training. The reason for this is twofold:

- The body has not been trained to sustain, for example, a Zone 5 effort if the race pace training was done in Zone 4.
- If nutrition is a factor in the race, the fuel taken in will burn up far quicker at a high intensity. If this is not accounted for during the nutrition planning, the athlete will hit the "wall."

With adrenaline pumping at the beginning of the swim or after coming off the bike, it can be easy to push at 100% without any regard for pacing. This is a common mistake amongst novices and elites. The athlete who races his or her own race will have the energy to give that final push in the last few miles of the run.

Strategy

Some athletes are strong in the swim but not the bike and run. Other athletes have a strong bike but poor swim. The key to triathlon is to maximize strengths and minimize weaknesses, which begins with training.

In a sprint distance race, the athlete can get away with small pacing errors. The race is short enough that the intensity can be ramped up to maximum for the entire duration in a "best effort" scenario. If there is concern about pacing a sprint distance race, a safe strategy is to build the effort across each discipline, where the run is the fastest in terms of relative effort.

The real pacing strategy begins in Olympic distance and above. Some simple cues can help an athlete work through a race to deliver a performance on par with the months of training leading into the race:

- **Swim relaxed and controlled**

There is little to be gained by swimming near maximum capacity. Elite amateurs and athletes with a swim background may be able to capitalize on a speedy swim, but most novices are best served airing on the side of "steady."

- **Utilize the bike to manage nutrition intake**

It is easiest to eat the planned nutrition on the bike due to ease of storage and ease of digestion. Set up a quick run by getting the calories in while pedaling.

- **"Flatten the course"**

By not pushing extra hard on uphills, bike, or run, the athlete can avoid costly spikes in intensity. Too many spikes can lift the heart rate to a point where it may not come back down. Instead, utilize downhills to showcase speed.

- **Run "guilty" easy**

The first mile/kilometer of the run should be used as a chance to gather thoughts and shake the "jelly legs" feeling that is common. This feeling lasts only about a mile before starting to find some running legs. Even with conscious control of pace, it is common to be still running quite fast out of transition, so don't sweat it if it feels "guilty"! It will pay dividends in the final miles.

- **Push!**

Even if the athlete was smart at the beginning of the run, the end of the race is going to be hard. This is the time to call upon the months of training, dig deep, and throw caution to the wind.

Chapter Review

This chapter covered basic pointers to help an athlete get started with swimming, cycling, and running. Some of these pointers included:

- Comfort in the water
- Swim techniques such as body position, breathing, and pulling
- Swimming in open water
- Getting accustomed to riding a bike on the road
- Understanding the mechanical limitations of running
- How to improve running technique
- General pacing and racing skills

With an understanding of what gear to purchase and what technical aspects to focus on, the athlete is now ready to understand some basic training terminology. The terms in **Chapter 5** are important regardless of whether the athlete has a coach or not.

Chapter 5: Training Terminology

Tip 28: By the numbers

While an athlete does not need an exercise physiology degree to get started in the sport of triathlon, some basic understanding of what to track during training is important. For example, many athletes train by heart rate, and more advanced athletes incorporate bike power (watts) and pace data with heart rate to develop a robust profile of training data.

Data is not meant to be confusing. It is meant to guide the training process and add structure. Successful athletes have structured programs, but successful athletes are also not a slave to the data. Numbers are only useful if the athlete can make sense of what they mean, whether that is with the help of a coach or on his or her own.

The following looks at the most popular metric used in triathlon: heart rate data.

Tip 29: Heart rate training

Heart rate training is a highly recommended practice when preparing for a triathlon. It relies on tracking the heart beats per minute (bpm) during a session via a chest strap or wrist-base monitor mentioned in Chapter 3. The chest strap is the gold standard, as wrist-based models are subject to error. If an athlete wants to make use of heart rate data, good data acquisition is important.

Using heart rate during training is only useful if there is context behind the number of beats per minute. Therefore, athletes are often set up with a target "zone" structure to follow. Certain zones correspond to certain intensities, and certain intensities correspond to certain physiological adaptations necessary for preparing for the demands of a race.

Furthermore, heart rate zones for each sport within the triathlon may be different. For example, an athlete may have the ability to achieve higher heart rates while running than while cycling due to the nature of the activity, i.e., running involves more of the musculature than cycling. This distinction is worth noting.

Alternative to swim heart rate tracking

Swimming can pose a difficult situation when trying to train via heart rate. Not all chest straps are waterproof; if they are, they can be uncomfortable to swim with. Additionally, the classic method of using two fingers on the jugular to measure heart rate manually is prone to error.

In this case, most athletes resort to using swim pace as the preferred way to track swimming intensity zones and structure the training accordingly. More information on setting zones is covered in **Tip 30**.

Tip 30: What are training zones?

As previously mentioned, setting heart rate training zones is a means of providing context to the athlete's training program. In addition, understanding which heart rate zone corresponds to which intensity level can help the athlete learn the difference in sensation between easy and hard training, a topic covered more in-depth in Chapter 5.

Many athletes train via a 5-one model, but other models are also used.

Tip 31: Setting zones

Heart rate zones are expressed as a percentage of the maximum heart rate. It was long thought that to determine maximum heart rate, one could use the formula of 220-your age. However, this method is subject to error and may only provide an estimate.

To determine an appropriate maximum heart rate, an athlete will need to test. Testing is one of the best ways to find out any training data metric for an athlete who has never done a race. Another way, for a more experienced athlete, is to use race data as it is common to be going at maximum intensity during a shorter distance race. Longer distance races may not be conducive to finding maximum heart rate.

Tip 32: Performing tests

Each sport within the triathlon warrants its own test, and this should make sense, given that each sport likely has its own maximum heart rate. Below are ideas for how to test for each sport. Of course, other tests can be used, but these are some of the simpler versions that an athlete can conduct independently.

Swim zone test protocol

Depending on the athlete's swim ability level, there are a few options, but the idea remains the same. This protocol relies on pace rather than heart rate due to the difficulties with consistently tracking swim heart rate. A pace zone model will result from this test. For both ability levels, a sufficient warmup of 500-1000 yards or meters is recommended.

- Beginner: 1000-yard or 800-meter best effort. Record time and then find the average pace per 100 yards or 100 meters. This pace will be referred to as the threshold pace. The threshold should make up the bulk of the high-intensity training with some efforts faster than the threshold
- Advanced: 2000-yard or meter best effort. Record time and then find the average pace per 100 yards or 100 meters. This pace will be referred to as the threshold pace. The threshold should make up the bulk of the high-intensity training with some efforts faster than the threshold.

The pace derived from this swim test can be fit to the 5-Zone model (see **Tip 32**), much like with heart rate zones.

Bike zone test protocol

Chapter 3 recommended the investment in an indoor cycling bike. This bike test protocol is a great use case for such equipment. The test can be performed on the road, but it is essential that the athlete is mindful of traffic and road furniture.

- A sufficient warmup of about 10-15 minutes of very light pedaling is recommended.
- The test begins with a 5-minute segment at an easy effort level.
- Every 5 minutes, the athlete will begin a new step and work at an effort level sufficient to raise heart rate by 10-15 bpm.
- The test continues until failure, and the final 5-minute step should be an all-out effort, thus providing a maximum heart rate value.
- The maximum heart rate is used to determine the training zones.

*It should be noted that this is a protocol to be used if the athlete does not have a power meter. For more info on how to perform a zone test with a power meter, there are numerous sources online that provide a similar test protocol to the one above.

Run zone test protocol

- A sufficient warmup of about a mile or more is recommended.
- After warming up, the athlete will run one lap moderate, one lap hard, and one lap at maximum effort on an oval track or measured section of road.
- No rest is to be taken between the laps, and the final lap is designed to elicit a maximal heart rate response.
- The maximum heart rate is then determined and can be used to derive the training zones.

The aforementioned tests are not the only means by which an athlete can find maximum heart rate or threshold pace. These are popular methods that are practical for the athlete to implement.

Tip 33: *Defining the five zones*

Zones 1-5 have strict definitions as it pertains to the heart rate response, but it is also valuable for the athlete to learn cues for how these efforts should feel.

Zone 1 training

Zone 1 is commonly referred to as the "easy zone." It is defined in most literature as 50-60% of the maximum heart rate determined by the testing protocol. The athlete can accumulate significant time in this zone as it is low-intensity work. Much of the **base phase** is geared toward working in Zone 1. A simple cue for an athlete running or cycling is that Zone 1 should be easy enough to carry on a conversation.

Zone 2 training

Zone 2 is a slight step up from Zone 1, defined as 60-70% of the maximum heart rate, and should still be regarded as relatively light in intensity. The athlete should be able to carry on a conversation like in Zone 1, but breathing may deepen with longer duration activity. As the athlete becomes more fit, the amount of work able to be done in Zone 2 can increase—to an extent *see **Tip 36**. Until then, a safe bet is to operate in Zone 1 or the lower end of the Zone 2 range. Recovery from both Zone 1 and Zone 2 work should not require much time, and the athlete can string together multiple days of this type of training.

Zone 3 training

Zone 3 training is defined as 70-80% of maximum heart rate and can be thought of as a moderate intensity level. It is generally regarded as the "gray zone" because there is a significant energy cost for not much gain at this intensity level. However, it can be quite easy for an athlete to operate in this zone because it does not feel extremely taxing and can often leave an athlete feeling like he or she got a "good workout."

Most beginner athletes would benefit from keeping time in this zone to a minimum. However, Zone 3 is a required part of the training if the athlete's event is a long-distance race that is often raced in this intensity zone. Race demands always reign supreme in this case.

If the athlete is targeting a sprint or Olympic distance race, where the race intensity is far above Zone 3, it would be more beneficial to spend time either in Zone 1 or 2, with intense work in Zone 4 and 5. Zone 3 may incur a recovery cost that impedes the ability to complete planned higher-intensity sessions successfully.

Zone 4 training

Commonly referred to as "threshold," Zone 4 is defined as 80-90% of the maximum heart rate. The work done in this zone is heavy, and the athlete should organize the training into multiple intervals of threshold followed by a period of easy Zone 1, e.g., 5 minutes threshold, 2 minutes Zone 1.

For an athlete looking to complete any distance of triathlon, the threshold can make up a significant portion of the intense sessions that are completed leading into a race. Due to its heavy nature, work in this zone should not be performed every day, and an intelligent training plan typically includes only one or two days per week of threshold work as the athlete works through the **Build phase** and **Race specific phase**. Details on phases are covered at length in **Chapter 6**.

Zone 5 training

The highest zone in the model, Zone 5, is defined as 90-100% of the maximum heart rate. This zone is severely taxing but can be beneficial for increasing an athlete's capacity to race at high intensities. To achieve a training effect, Zone 5 can only be maintained for a few minutes at a time during a training session. An athlete typically organizes the training into multiple short intervals like threshold training. Within an overall training plan, the amount of work done in Zone 5 is a small contribution.

Tip 34: Other training metrics to track

Training via pace

If an athlete is unable or unwilling to acquire a heart rate monitor, training by pace can be effective. Pace is a popular metric in swimming, and most swimming workouts are structured according to pace.

In running, pace zones are useful for determining intensity as it pertains to a goal race time. For example, if an athlete wants to complete the run portion of a sprint triathlon (3.1 mi/5km) in 20 minutes, then the goal pace per mile would need to be about 6:26/mi, and per km would need to be 4:00/km. Many athletes organize a running interval workout according to the goal pace to accumulate time at the desired pace.

Time at pace is valuable for understanding the feel of differing intensities. When paired with heart rate feedback, pace data can help build an athlete's understanding of how his or her physiology is responding to training.

One of the major drawbacks of training exclusively by pace is that running often involves variable terrain. An athlete may have difficulty keeping a consistent pace due to the up-and-down nature of hilly terrain. This is a situation where heart rate training would be preferred, but pace training is not to be completely discounted.

Cycling is nearly impossible to train according to pace as terrain varies the speed of the bike and rider too much to hold a long-term, consistent speed.

Training via power

In cycling, it is common for training to be guided via the use of a power meter. A power meter measures the amount of strain a cyclist puts through the bike's drivetrain or into the pedals and displays this number in watts, a measure of power. With power, an athlete can understand how much mechanical work is being done during a bike ride. This can be useful for developing target race intensities or training zones similar to heart rate.

Much like pace-based training, power used in conjunction with heart rate is a powerful tool for gathering data that is key for understanding improvements in fitness. However, power meters are quite expensive, as mentioned in **Chapter 3**, and the learning curve with power-based training is an advanced topic. Therefore, most first-time triathletes would be best served performing cycling training with heart rate alone. In fact, many athletes have gone on to be successful in triathlons without the use of a power meter on the bike.

Tip 35: Context is key

The following are a few "rules" that apply to training structure when using a zone model. It is important that the athlete understands the context of the zones to develop the ability to self-regulate during a build-up to a race.

Tip 36: Working in your zones

After a successful test to set the zones, a good rule of thumb is to operate at the bottom half of the zone during general endurance sessions. This affords the athlete an opportunity to spend long durations at the desired intensity because he or she is not pushing the upper limits of the zone. Ideally, the line between Zone 1 and 2 should be an intensity the athlete can sustain "all day long."

The intensity control becomes more important as the athlete approaches race day and begins more Zone 4 and 5 work. However, just because the athlete can straddle the line between Zone 4 and Zone 5 during a workout does not always indicate that is what should be done. This can impair recovery, a topic covered in **Chapter 8**.

Tip 37: A note on Zone 2

As the athlete becomes fitter, the pace or power at the determined Zone 2 heart rate should be faster. That is a byproduct of endurance training, and to some extent, this is an ideal adaptation. The caveat is that the overall output at this heart rate will increase; thus, the amount of physical work being done also increases.

The metabolic system determines how many carbohydrates and how much fat is used for fuel during exercise. As a result, carbohydrate fuel storage is limited, whereas fat is essentially unlimited.

Given that it is common for novice athletes to develop the aerobic system rapidly but have a lagging metabolic system, performing upper Zone 2 work can be too reliant on carbohydrates, a limited fuel source. The metabolic system takes time to adapt and improve. In this case, the safe bet for training is to stick with the bottom half of the determined zone and extend duration rather than increase intensity. The ability to go long pays dividends at all levels of triathlon. First, do it. Then, do it longer. Then, do it more intensely.

Tip 38: Do not compare

Each athlete is an individual when it comes to heart rate zones. Therefore, there is little utility in one athlete comparing zones to a friend, teammate, or even a professional athlete.

Tip 39: Retesting

While the idea of testing may seem esoteric and scientific, it is an important part of the process. It is impossible to know if something has improved without testing for it.

For a clear picture of improvements in fitness and performance, retesting must occur. At a minimum, testing at the beginning of training for an event is best practice, but it is recommended that data is updated every 6-8 weeks.

Maximum heart rate will likely remain unchanged in the weeks leading into a triathlon race, so if training only by heart rate, an athlete may not need to retest.

However, if the athlete has integrated pace or power data into the program, retesting can reveal fitness adaptations necessary for improvement. Updates can then be made to the zones to continue to take more steps forward in the training program.

Chapter Review

This chapter covered the following:

- Data in the training program
- The basics of heart rate training
- Finding maximum heart rate via testing and setting heart rate training zones from the test
- Ideas for testing protocols for swimming, cycling, running
- An explanation for each of the five zones in the 5-Zone training model
- Other metrics commonly tracked alongside heart rate, such as pace and power
- Recommendations for athletes when working in the determined zones

Training zones are only useful if they are part of a well-structured training plan. **Chapter 6** dives into creating a program that will render the athlete successful on race day.

Chapter 6: The Basics of Training

Tip 40: Developing a program

Training is the meat and potatoes of preparation for a triathlon. An athlete must do the work. Some athletes decide to be self-coached, while others seek out professional assistance in the form of a coach or purchasing an online plan. Regardless, the smart athlete will follow a periodized and progressive program that builds fitness to deliver the athlete to the start line ready to go. What exactly do periodized and progressive mean?

Tip 41: Periodized and progressive

The purpose of using a periodized model is to gradually introduce new stimuli to the body to get the best possible training effect. Focusing only on one element of training neglects all of the important aspects needed to deliver a successful performance on race day. This requires a mix of long, short, easy, and hard, at specific times throughout a race preparation with a careful eye on recovery.

If the prescription for training is adequate, the athlete will eventually adapt and be ready to progress. Progression includes slight overload in the form of more duration, total volume, intensity, or other metrics. It is recommended to only progress one element at a time, i.e., opting for more volume but keeping intensity low.

Adaptations are a manifestation of being fit, and being fit for the race demands is crucial for success in triathlon.

It is common practice for a training program to have different phases. Most periodization models follow this basic outline:

- Base phase
- Build phase
- Race-specific phase

- Taper phase

Tip 42: Base phase

Much like a race car, the athlete will want to have the most efficient engine possible. This begins with the base phase. Most of the training in this phase is done at a slow pace or a low intensity.

Aerobic is the name of the game, meaning that the athlete is working at an intensity that can be sustained for hours at a time. The preferred fuel source for this type of activity comes from fat, and humans store far more fat than carbohydrates. Therefore, carbohydrate is the preferred fuel for anaerobic activity, which is what the bulk of the intense training involves. An athlete should spend the longest amount of time in the training preparation in the base phase. Since it is not imperative that the training is specific to the race demands, an athlete can work in the base phase for months before progressing to the next portion of the periodized model. The subsequent phases are time sensitive, as an athlete can only hold peak form and fitness for a few weeks at a time.

Training via heart rate in running or cycling or by pace in swimming is the easiest way to gain objective feedback for adhering to a specific intensity domain, i.e., hard or easy. More details on easy vs. hard are covered later in this chapter under **Tip 51**.

Tip 43: Build phase

A proper base phase of multiple months will yield improvements in efficiency, but efficiency is only part of the equation when training for a triathlon. The athlete, no matter the race distance, will need durability to hold steady throughout the race.

Enter the build phase. If the athlete has chosen a specific race, this phase can begin 12-16 weeks before the target event. Again, more anaerobic or high-intensity training is included in the program at the expense of the high volumes of low intensity seen in the Base phase.

It is important for this phase to follow a progression model so that the athlete becomes strategically overloaded, such that the body adapts to the overload and improvements in fitness are realized. Progression is typically planned in a linear fashion across the 12-16 weeks, and regular recovery periods are worked into the build phase, allowing the athlete a chance to absorb the progress and then continue building. A worked example using a weekly long run may look as follows:

- Week 1: 5-mile-long run
- Week 2: 6-mile-long run
- Week 3: 7-mile-long run
- Week 4: Recovery period; may include no long run or a shortened version (~5 miles)
- Week 5: 6-mile-long run
- Week 6: 7-mile-long run
- Week 7: 8-mile-long run
- Week 8: Recovery period; may include no long run or a *new* shortened version (~6 miles).

The idea with the progression is that the long run is being progressed in the context of the other training. Elements of the swim and the bike are likely to be progressing in a similar fashion.

Beyond the 8-week mark, the long run may continue to increase in distance, increase in intensity, or level off for a period of maintenance. The decision of how best to progress is predicated on how the athlete is responding to the planned training. For example, if the athlete is struggling with the 6-mile long run in week two from the example, it is worth looking at how the swim and bike training is going and making changes to foster a well-rounded performance.

The athlete may simply be at a point where it is justified to repeat a week instead of adding more. Progressive overload is needed to induce change, but excessive overload should be avoided.

Tip 44: Race-specific phase

The race-specific phase normally lasts 2-4 weeks. It precedes the **Taper phase,** the athlete's opportunity to gain valuable insight into how to operate at race intensity. The general conditioning built up during the **Base phase** is crucial for making the race pace sessions constructive rather than destructive. The base supports all other training.

Some athletes prefer to insert a short race early in this phase. Racing can key the athlete into areas that need improvement before the target event. It is recommended that 4-6 weeks are placed between the tune-up race and the target event, but some prefer to race as close as two weeks before. It is a matter of preference. An athlete targeting an Olympic distance race may enter a sprint distance race to practice racing skills and gain an understanding of where race-specific fitness is at.

If the target event is the only planned event for the athlete, which is likely the case for a first-time triathlete, a practice race simulation can be useful. Race simulations are not sanctioned races but allow for practicing racing skills and "revving the race engine," so to speak. The simulation can be set up in the normal training environment.

Often, an athlete will make mental notes of mistakes made or may discover that they are more fatigued than expected from the prior weeks of training. In this case, the athlete sees the need for freshening up and will enter the next phase, the **Taper phase.**

Tip 45: Taper phase

This phase is, in theory, the most straightforward phase of the periodized plan, but it is subject to much debate in the triathlon community.

Taper is the gradual "tapering off" of training volume and intensity to absorb all the hard work done in the weeks prior to the event. The intent is to afford the athlete a chance to freshen up and feel great. Seems easy, right? However, each athlete is different, and this is where the great debate lies.

Some athletes prefer a taper that lasts a few *weeks*, while others swear by only bringing the training down a few *days* before.

There are not many hard and fast rules to tapering, but a few guidelines for the athlete looking to compete in his or her first triathlon may be helpful:

- Some of the reduction in training provides a **mental edge** for succeeding on the day.
- Some **fitness** is lost in the taper process, but this is intentional, and the gains made in **freshness** do outweigh the losses in fitness.
- **Intensity** often stays high during taper, but the total amount of intensity in the weeks or days of taper is **less than the normal** volume.
- Base or general aerobic training makes up a small sliver of the athlete's training during this time. The focus is either on **executing important sessions or resting**. Gaining fitness is not a goal during taper.

One rule that is particularly helpful for some triathletes is that ten days before the event, there are no more gains in fitness to be made. You are stuck with what you have got! This advice can ease the mind of the anxious athlete and prevent them from doing too much during the taper period. If one thing is for sure during taper, it is doing more will not be helpful for competing and succeeding on race day. **So relax.** The work has been done!

Tip 46: Block periodization

A more advanced topic, block periodization, is commonly used by triathletes. Blocks refer to a set number of days in which an athlete is focused on accumulating work, followed by a short recovery period. Typically, a block has a specific focus, such as increasing the amount of cycling or improving run speed.

A block may be as long as six weeks or as short as three days. The duration of the block depends greatly on the athlete's fitness goal. The longer blocks are defined as mesocycles, and the shorter blocks are defined as microcycles. Sometimes multiple microcycles can comprise a larger mesocycle.

Terminology aside, the block model can be effective for structuring daily training for an athlete, especially in triathlon, where it is difficult to place focus on all three sports all the time. Periodizing in this manner requires a firm understanding of one's physiology. It is recommended to have spent time in the sport or in other endurance sports before incorporating block periodization.

Tip 47: *Applying the phases*

The periodized plan involves a mix of swimming, cycling, and running training. This is especially important in the race-specific phase, when workouts are often grouped. For example, a bike followed by a run, in close succession, usually at high intensity. The bike-to-run or swim-to-bike workouts are referred to as "brick' workouts in the community. The idea is to help prepare the athlete for race day demands.

Most of the training per sport is not done as a brick workout but rather in isolation. The following provides some general guidelines for swimming, cycling, and running to complete each week. Three sports in one requires some careful planning!

Tip 48: *How much of each sport to do per week?*

At a minimum, an athlete needs to complete one swim, one bike, and one run during the week to be familiar with the race demands. However, far more volume and frequency are recommended.

For the average amateur triathlete, aiming to adhere to 3-5 sessions per sport per week is a good rule of thumb. Most athletes would benefit greatly from consistently logging weeks of three swims, three rides, and three runs. Nine total workouts in a week, when strategically planned and placed, is a time lean strategy that works for many. For those looking to associate this 3x3 protocol with a time commitment, it may yield 7-10 hours per week in total.

If an athlete is keen on taking on a longer distance, such as the Half Ironman, more training will be needed to fit the race demands. Furthermore, Ironman training is an advanced-level topic that is only touched on briefly later in this book. It is a format of the sport that behaves differently from the other distances and incurs a more substantial time and energy cost. It would not be recommended to use the 3x3 protocol for an Ironman preparation, but some athletes have become quite fit off of smaller volumes of work. Nothing is impossible.

Tip 49: The frequency model

The more often an athlete can engage in triathlon-specific activities, the better. Shorter and more frequent sessions allow for faster recovery to come back and repeat the sessions again the next day. This is known as the frequency model and is preferred because it lends itself to making an athlete more consistent.

There is a time and place for long, massive days, especially in the longer distance training. There is also a time and place for training with lingering fatigue to foster an adaptation. However, the frequency model is an excellent guidepost for a busy, working, amateur triathlete looking to get to a start line fit and healthy. The needle must slowly be pushed toward doing more instead of violently ramping up the workload. Remember, you have to make it to the line without injury or illness even to have a chance at competing and succeeding!

Tip 50: Workout types

Following the basic 3x3 protocol from above, an athlete can expect three basic sessions per sport during the week:

Swimming:

The long swim

The long swim is a staple in the triathlete's weekly schedule as it can build general aerobic fitness without the muscular demand in the legs seen in cycling or running. The athlete will want to complete a volume and duration of swimming longer than the other swims during the week but keep the intensity in Zone 1 or Zone 2 category. For athletes targeting a longer distance race, becoming familiar with fatigue in the upper body is important. The long swim can be a way of building muscular resilience in the arms, shoulders, and trunk. Furthermore, if an athlete has access to open water such as a lake or ocean bay, the long swim is a great opportunity to practice swimming like at a race venue. Most triathlon swims do not take place in a pool.

The short, technique-focused swim

Short, technique-focused swims are intended to improve an athlete's efficiency. Sound technical skill is arguably the most important element to becoming a competent swimmer. These swims can be inserted on an easy day as a recovery-type activity. Neither speed nor distance is the name of the game here. The intensity level typically does not exceed Zone 1 or Zone 2.

The short, speed-focused swim

To swim fast, the athlete must swim fast. Many races begin with a mass start, and the more speed an athlete has to get out in front of the large pack to avoid swimming over others, the better. However, this is not the only reason for training in swim speed. Swimming can be a major source of cardiovascular fitness without the impact risk of running. Speed swims can incorporate long bouts of Zone 4 efforts and short 25-yard/meter sprints that are at the peak of the Zone 5 range. While swimming may not win the race for an athlete, making the adaptations necessary to swim well without excessive fatigue can play an important role in the bike and run portion of the race.

Cycling:

The long ride

The long ride is a staple in the athlete's weekly training, especially in the **Base phase**. The purpose of the long ride is to make improvements in the aerobic economy, thus supporting the more intense training yet to come. The duration of the long ride may be only 90 minutes for a less experienced athlete or more than 5 hours for an Ironman athlete. Most long rides are steady, conversational-paced efforts in Zone 1 or Zone 2. Longer distance athletes may have specific Zone 3 efforts within a long ride in the **Build** or **Race-specific** phases.

The standard ride

The standard ride is just how it sounds. A steady effort within the Zone 2 limits may take between 1 and 2 hours. Athletes targeting longer races may find time for a few of these rides throughout a week but sticking to the 3x3 protocol for a beginner amateur, there is only room for one of these rides. Once race-specific preparation begins, this ride may take on the role of a short recovery ride or a second intense ride. This is dependent on an athlete's overall plan.

The intense ride

Hard bike riding is a requirement for an athlete to make the necessary adaptation for running well afterward. The intense ride need not be a long affair, but most of the time during the ride is spent in Zone 4 or Zone 5 in the form of intervals. A sprint distance athlete may do 5x3 minutes as hard as they can, with 3 minutes of Zone 1 in between, for example. There are multiple ways to organize a hard training ride, and some athletes prefer to forego intervals altogether in favor of a group ride. These rides serve as ad hoc races and, while fun, can be quite taxing. It is recommended first to understand the demands of a group ride and how it fits the overall training plan before choosing it over a controlled interval session.

Running:

The long run

The long run is yet again a staple in the athlete's weekly training. It is designed to improve the aerobic economy and give the athlete valuable "time on feet." The overall intensity of this run is typically done in Zone 1 or Zone 2, but as always, quality components may be integrated as a race becomes closer. In addition, the overall distance of a long run is dependent on the target race distance. For example, a sprint distance athlete may only be doing 5-7 miles for a long run, while an Ironman athlete may do 20 miles.

A speed workout (track or hills)

Running fast is one activity that harbors an injury risk. Hard running is not to be done too often and only when the athlete has demonstrated sufficient progress in the **Base phase**. Speed workouts can be done on an oval track, on hills, on the road, or on a treadmill. The purpose is to work in Zones 3, 4, and 5 to build specific fitness for racing, typically in the form of intervals or sustained periods bookended by a warmup and cooldown. A sprint distance athlete may warmup for 10 minutes, complete 5x400 meter repeats at goal race intensity, and then cool down for 10 minutes, for example.

A short, easy run

Short, easy runs take on a few roles. They allow the athlete to accumulate more running volume without risking injury like with a speed run. The 3x3 protocol only affords the athlete one of these runs per week, but athletes with more time or a need for higher volume running may complete 2 or 3 of these easy runs during the week.

Off the bike!

A favorite of many, the off-the-bike run is just how it sounds. It is a run done directly after a bike ride to simulate running after cycling in a race. The run off the bike can be a valuable source of information for how running feels after riding or if the fueling strategy is working for the athlete. Depending on the training phase, it may be an easy run, or it may be a race pace run. The community refers to this as a "brick" workout, and there is no consensus on how that term came to be. Some say it is because the legs feel like bricks and others say it is because two workouts back-to-back are like stacking bricks!

Off the bike can also be a time-savvy strategy for an athlete who needs to ride and run but cannot devote a second session to running later or earlier in the day.

*More specific workout ideas are outlined in the index, **Chapter 11**, and cover some staple workouts for each distance of the triathlon race.*

Tip 51: Putting it in practice with a worked example

Training is a highly individual process, but a novice athlete can benefit greatly from seeing a weekly schedule laid out in detail.

The following is a recommended structure during the **Build phase** for an athlete targeting a sprint or Olympic distance race. **The build phase** was the chosen point in the periodization because this is a time when all zones of training are featured in the program, and some race specificity is present. This allows the athlete to see a full spectrum example of training. The athlete must spend the recommended 8-12 weeks in the **Base phase** to accumulate general fitness before jumping into a plan like in the example.

The example follows the 3x3 protocol for training structure because that structure is a surefire way to maintain consistency in training.

Week 1

Monday	Tuesday	Wednesday	Thursday	Friday	Saturday	Sunday
Swim	**Bike**	**Swim**	**Run**	**Swim**	**Bike**	**Run**
45 min	75 min	1 hour	45 min	45 min	2 hours	1 hour
Technique	Intense	Long	Speed	Speed	Long	Long
400 WU	20 min warmup	500 mixed warmup	15 min warmup	400 warmup	2 hours steady Zone 2	1 hour progression as 30 min Zone 1 + 30 min Zone 2
4x100 pulling :15 seconds rest	5x5 min Zone 4 with 2 min Zone 1 between each	6x300 steady :30 seconds rest	4x800 meters or 0.5 miles Zone 4 with 1 minute Zone 1 between	300 steady	**Run**	
4x50 breathing every 3	5x alternate 30 seconds Zone 5 and 30 seconds Zone 1	100 easy	3x200 meters Zone 5+ with 1 min Zone 1 between	200 pulling	**30 minutes**	
------		6x200 steady :20 seconds rest		10x50 fastest possible average :30 seconds rest between	Standard	
100	15 min Zone 1 + 2 cooldown	100 easy	10-15 minutes Zone 1 cooldown	200 easy	20-30 minutes of easy Zone 1 + 2	
150		**Bike**		10x25 fastest possible average :15 seconds rest between	*Can be done as off the bike	
200		1 hour				
150		Standard				
100		1 hour easy Zone 1 + 2				
All steady with :15 seconds rest						
4x50 breathing every 3						

Totals in hours

<u>Swim:</u> 2hr 30 min <u>Bike:</u> 4hr 15 min <u>Run:</u> 2hr 15 min <u>Overall:</u> 9 hours

Week 2

Monday	Tuesday	Wednesday	Thursday	Friday	Saturday	Sunday
Swim	**Bike**	**Swim**	**Run**	**Swim**	**Bike**	**Run**
45 min	**75 min**	**1 hour**	**45 min**	**45 min**	**2 hours 15 min**	**1 hour**
<u>Technique</u>	<u>Intense</u>	<u>Long</u>	<u>Speed</u>	<u>Speed</u>	<u>Long</u>	<u>Long</u>
400 WU	20 min warmup	500 mixed warmup	15 min warmup	400 warmup	2 hours 15 min steady Zone 2	1 hour progression as 30 min Zone 1 + 30 min Zone 2
5x100 pulling :15 seconds rest	6x5 min Zone 4 with 2 min Zone 1 between each	4x400 steady :30 seconds rest	3x1600 meters or 1.0 miles Zone 4 with 2 minutes Zone 1 between	300 steady		
4x50 breathing every 3	5x alternate 30 seconds Zone 5 and 30 seconds Zone 1	100 easy	3x200 meters Zone 5+ with 1 min Zone 1 between	200 pulling		
------		4x300 steady :20 seconds rest		15x50 fastest possible average :30 seconds rest between	**Run**	
100		100 easy		200 easy	**30 min**	
150	10 min Zone 1 + 2 cooldown	**Bike**	10-15 minutes Zone 1 cooldown	15x25 fastest possible average :15 seconds rest between	<u>Standard</u>	
200		**1 hour**			20-30 minutes of easy Zone 1 + 2	
150		<u>Standard</u>				
100		1 hour easy Zone 1 + 2			*Can be done as off the bike	
<u>All steady</u>						
4x50 breathing every 3						

Totals in hours

<u>Swim:</u> 2hr 30 min <u>Bike:</u> 4hr 30 min <u>Run:</u> 2hr 15 min <u>Overall:</u> 9 hours 15 min

Week 3

Monday	Tuesday	Wednesday	Thursday	Friday	Saturday	Sunday
Swim	**Bike**	**Swim**	**Run**	**Swim**	**Bike**	**Run**
45 min	75 min	1 hour	45 min	45 min	2.25 hours	70 min
Technique	Intense	Long	Standard	Speed	Long	Long
400 WU	20 min warmup	500 mixed warmup	45 min Zone 1 + 2	400 warmup	2.25 hours steady Zone 2	70 min progressions as 30 min Zone 1 + 30 min Zone 2 + 10 min Zone 1 + 2
5x100 pulling :15 seconds rest	6x6 min Zone 4 with 2 min Zone 1 between each	2x500 steady :30 seconds rest		300 steady	**Run**	
4x50 breathing every 3	10 min Zone 1 + 2 cooldown	100 easy		200 pulling	30 min	
5x100 pulling :15 seconds rest		3x400 steady :20 seconds rest		25 fast	Speed	
		100 easy		50 fast	10 min Zone 4 + 5 min Zone 1 repeat x2	
4x50 breathing every 3		4x300 steady :10 seconds rest		75 fast	*Should be done as off the bike	
				100 fast		
		Bike		75 fast		
		1 hour		50 fast		
		Standard		25 fast		
		1 hour easy Zone 1 + 2		100 easy		
				Repeat x2		

Totals in hours

<u>Swim:</u> 2hr 30 min <u>Bike:</u> 4hr 30 min <u>Run:</u> 2hr 25 min <u>Overall:</u> 9 hours 25 min

The total duration of miles covered may vary depending on the ability of the athlete, but the framework is the same. Training based on relative intensity according to the zones set up in the recommended testing from **Chapter 5** makes each plan unique. The recommendations in the sample plan can be adjusted to fit the athlete's schedule. Flexibility is key for the amateur athlete.

Tip 52: Hard vs. Easy training

A common misconception in the endurance world is that progress is made only through hard training. This could not be further from the truth. A careful balance between intense sessions and easy sessions is required to make the necessary adaptations.

Hard training is stressful

The idea of doing an intense session, such as one that may be performed in the **Race-specific phase**, is to properly stress the body so that the athlete becomes resilient to the demands of the race. That is the simplest explanation of building specific fitness.

The stress from intense workouts does come with a cost. It is imperative that the athlete understands other stressors, such as work or family obligations so that the hard work is not overly taxing on the athlete's body. Training stress is only a small slice of an athlete's life.

Hard training can be effective in small quantities

If an athlete is heavily involved in work or family life, the amount of training stress he or she can undergo is limited. If this is concerning to you, do not fret. A little bit of liveliness in the program goes a long way to keep the athlete turning over.

As a rule of thumb, sticking to 80% of the training in the easy domain and 20% in the hard domain will get an athlete where they want to be athletically while keeping them healthy and able to contribute to other areas of life. Furthermore, a 90% easy to 10%

hard split is still a safe bet for the athlete who lives a particularly stressful non-training life.

What is hard?

Objectively, if an athlete has a "hard" or intense session on the training menu, this usually means the work is being performed in Zone 4 or Zone 5. However, it should not be overlooked that a large training day spent mostly in Zone 2 and Zone 3 can be equally or even more stressful than a short and hard Zone 5 session. This is where training load becomes an important factor to monitor and will be discussed in depth in **Chapter 8,** the recovery chapter.

What is easy?

Just as a short and hard session can be stressful, a properly performed long and easy session can be helpful for building an athlete's fitness without taking too much away from the other training days during the week. The definition of easy is loosely tied to the Zone 1 and Zone 2 domain, but it can also apply to the overall feeling the athlete has during the training session. It is important to blend feelings with objective metrics to understand true training intensity. Sometimes hard feels effortless! That does not mean that it was truly easy, however. Everything has a cost in the training world.

Easy—where the rubber meets the road

Training at a low intensity can be done frequently. This plays along with the important concept of the frequency model and allows the athlete to accumulate the training duration necessary to build a base. Without an aerobic base, the athlete increases his or her chance of coming up short in having a successful experience in a triathlon. A robust base also improves recovery from intense training. This, of course, is if injury or illness has not tripped the athlete up already due to training too intensely too frequently. Frequency is important, but only when there is a balance of hard and easy. Always hard, every day blunts adaptation.

Tip 53: Load vs. recover

A simple way for an athlete to split up a week or an entire preparation for an event is to categorize training days into loading days and recovery days. There should be days in the schedule where it is acceptable to go big, go long, or go hard. These are loading days, and it is intentional. There should also be days when the athlete keeps it light in terms of duration and intensity. There is also a time and a place for maintenance activity where the athlete is neither doing a recovery day nor looking to achieve overload. All three types of days are part of a training plan.

Blindly working as hard as possible until the athlete's body no longer wants to is a common mishap. Triathletes love to work hard and adopt the "more is more" mantra. More work should equate to more fitness, and it does to an extent. It is when the athlete is doing too much work that the result is undesirable.

Aiming to stay healthy and slightly less fit rather than pushing to the absolute limit and risking it all is a safer approach. Overtraining will result in many more recovery days than if the athlete was slightly undertrained and able to do loading or maintenance days multiple times in a week or training block. Improvements in triathlon take time. Doing enough is often not the issue when training for a triathlon.

Chapter Review

This chapter covered the following:

- Developing a training program
- The definition of periodization and the subsequent training phases within the periodized model (base, build, race, taper)
- How to apply the phases
- Recommended training frequency per week for the average amateur depending on the distance of the race
- The all-important frequency model
- Recommended training structure

- Hard training compared to easy training and how to quantify "hard" and "easy"

Now that the athlete understands training methodology and how to structure a program using basic principles, it is time to introduce ways to enhance performance through diet and recovery. **Chapter 7** is a crash course on how an athlete should set up a diet to ensure he or she is well fueled and healthy.

Chapter 7: How to Eat

Tip 54: Importance of nutrition

There are no hacks or quick fixes in the sport of triathlon, but nutrition is one area that can greatly enhance an athlete's performance and overall well-being without any extra training. The food that an athlete eats is the fuel that is used during the many hours of training. Low-quality fuel leads to low-quality training, and low-quality training will not result in training, competing, and succeeding in triathlon. Nutrition is the 4th discipline.

Two domains of nutrition are important in the sport:

- the food eaten during a race/training
- the food eaten outside of a race/training.

A sprint distance athlete may not require supplementation of fuel during a race, but as race distances increase, a plan for taking in nutrition becomes increasingly important.

The food eaten outside of training, regardless of the level of the athlete, is crucial for improving overall body composition, metabolism, and aiding recovery from the demands of training.

Tip 55: Human metabolism—a quick overview

On a scientific level, metabolism is defined as the conversion of food intake into usable energy for the body. This usable energy powers basic homeostatic processes like breathing, heart function, and brain function. It also allows the body to use energy voluntarily, such as in exercise or training.

In a basic human diet, three macromolecules exist: protein, fat, and carbohydrate. All three play an important role in the athlete's training pursuits, whether for fuel or for recovery.

Fat and carbohydrate are the two primary fuel sources during exercise. Given that triathlon training is deeply rooted in aerobic training, the preferred fuel source is fat. When the training becomes more intense, perhaps above the aerobic zone, the fuel partitioning begins to shift toward more carbohydrate utilization. An athlete must be careful to perform aerobic training easily enough to not tap into the carbohydrate stores too deeply. Preserving these stores are important because carbohydrate storage is limited, whereas fat is a slow and long-burning fuel source that is unlikely to run out. Exercise is less energetically costly for an athlete with a well-trained fat metabolism.

It should now be apparent that in a race scenario, where intensity is high, supplementation with carbohydrates is key to avoiding an energy crash and a dip in performance. This is because when an athlete experiences a crash, the muscle has been depleted of glycogen. Glycogen is how carbohydrate is stored in the muscle and is drawn from when carbohydrates are to be used as fuel.

Ask any athlete who has miscalculated nutrition intake in training or in racing, and they will tell you that avoiding the energy crash or "bonk" is paramount. Whether it happens in a race or in training, there are typically downstream effects that are greater than feeling "out of energy." Recovery is impaired, injuries can occur, and the training effect is dampened.

Tip 56: Eat your protein!

Protein is essential to an endurance athlete. It is not so much a fuel source as it is a building block to maintaining health. Some of the main impacts of eating sufficient protein are as follows:

- Aids in the growth and repair of muscle tissue
- Curbs hunger and helps avoid going overboard on carbohydrate
- Aids in supporting the building blocks of a healthy immune system

Most athletes would benefit greatly from sticking to 0.8 grams to 1.0 grams per pound of body weight. In metric units, this is 1.6 grams to 2.0 grams per kilogram of body weight. Making protein intake a priority at meals or with snacks is a good habit for an athlete to develop.

Tip 57: *Food as nutrients*

Food is energy, but food is also nutrients. Nutrient-dense foods are ideal for eating outside of training as they provide the necessary nourishment for growth and repair. Fruits, vegetables, whole grains, and lean protein comprise the bulk of the nutrient-dense category. An athlete should prioritize food choices from this group before reaching for items from the energy-dense category. Energy-dense food high in sugar that processes easily is ideal for use before, during, and after training to keep the body out of an energy-depleted state. Sports nutrition products often fit this mold, but **Tip 68** will cover when and how to use sports nutrition properly.

Tip 58: *Fuel the training—What's the purpose?*

Triathlon training can harbor a serious energy demand, especially for longer distance athletes. Avoiding energy depletion is the key to rolling through many consistent weeks in a row and getting the race results that an athlete desires.

For a training session lasting one hour or less, it is usually not necessary to take any nutrition supplementation during the session. Eating a snack or meal before and replenishing afterward is plenty.

In sessions that range from 90-120 minutes, a drink or snack containing 30-60 grams of carbohydrates is standard practice. Sixty grams of carbohydrates per hour is a value that is well reported in the literature and can be applied to longer training sessions as well. Athletes competing in Half or Full distance Ironman events will regularly have 3+ hour sessions on the training menu. Some athletes do well with supplementing at 70, 80, 90, or even 100 grams per hour. The higher end of the carbohydrate intake range is usually reserved for a long *and* intense session or even a race.

Swim nutrition

It is difficult to take in solid food during a swim session; thus, a liquid form of calories is typically recommended. Most athletes will be able to get by having no calories during a swim, making sure to monitor intake before and after. However, if there is a run session or bike session soon to follow the swim, having liquid calories in the form of juice or sports drink products is a sound strategy to maintain energy levels throughout the training day.

Bike nutrition

The bike is the one discipline where eating is made easy. There is not much upper body movement like in swimming or up and down movement like running, so intake can be quite high. There is also easy storage of food either in bottles on the bike or in jersey pockets. The same carbohydrate intake rate of 60+ grams per hour remains for the bike.

A skill worth mastering on the bike is training the gut to handle a steady intake of carbohydrates. Many products are intended to be fast digesting, but if an athlete is unfamiliar with slamming 60-100 grams of carbohydrate in an hour for a few hours, it can result in cramping or vomiting once reaching the run portion. This is due to the body not being trained to have sufficient uptake capacity.

It is worth mentioning that an athlete competing in sprint distance or Olympic distance races may not need to be too concerned with training the gut. These races are typically short enough to get by using one or two sports drinks. It takes about two hours for the body to exhaust carbohydrate stores completely; thus, minimal supplementation, if any, is needed for races lasting 1-3 hours. The real eating contest begins in longer distance racing.

Run nutrition

If the athlete has worked consciously on training the gut, the nutrition intake on the run becomes less of an issue. Due to the up and down movement in running, liquid calories are often recommended to avoid any stomach "sloshing." This applies to both training and racing. Exceeding 60 grams of carbohydrates per hour on a run is an advanced-level skill, and most athletes try to stick to 30 grams at minimum. Avoiding gastrointestinal distress is crucial both in daily training and in a race.

Tip 59: Race Nutrition

A well-planned eating strategy that begins in the days before a race can give an athlete a significant boost on race day. A common tradition in endurance sports is to have a "carb load" period before a race. Many athletes take this to the extreme, cramming in plates of pasta the day (or night) before a race. In most cases, this is a recipe for a stomach ache and bloating the next morning. However, the "carb load" can be effective if done responsibly and usually can take place over the course of a few days where the total carbohydrate intake has been increased across the days as opposed to one day. Moreover, a reduction in training during the taper phase coupled with no change in carbohydrate intake can get an athlete in the ballpark of having sufficient glycogen stores if he or she is hesitant to ramp up the carbohydrates.

Tip 60: Don't change a thing Part 1

During the five days leading into a race, the athlete's diet should include no foods that were never eaten during the normal training. This mistake is more common than one would expect, but many races require travel and staying in a hotel where eating out is a quick option. If the restaurant does not have a meal option for keeping the diet normal, the athlete should make a grocery store trip to acquire foods that fit the normal diet. A GI issue in the days leading up to the race can rob the athlete of glycogen storage and impede electrolyte balance. Jamming loads of pizza or pasta down is not required and is, frankly, not advised unless the athlete has done this in the past with no impact on training or race performance.

Tip 61: *Spare the veggies*

Nutrient-dense foods are crucial in the athlete's diet, but pre-race is the one time when it is acceptable to slack on the vegetable intake. Keeping a low-fiber diet heading into a race can avoid uncomfortable bloat and digestive troubles. In the 48 hours before, it is recommended to keep the fiber at a minimum and focus on frequent small portions of meals such as rice and eggs, rice and chicken, or rice and a plant-based protein source if the athlete is plant-based.

Tip 62: *Race morning*

Many triathlon races begin early in the morning, requiring an abnormally early wake-up time for most. It is common for an athlete to not feel hungry at this time of the morning but having something to eat is essential. 3-4 hours before the gun goes off for the race is a common sweet spot for "breakfast," but two hours before can still be enough time to digest.

Longer distance athletes should aim for 800-1000 calories from low-GI foods—white toast and jam, rice and eggs, banana and toast, oatmeal, etc. The options are endless, and ideally, the athlete will have practiced this strategy before longer training days that were near race duration.

Sprint and Olympic distance athletes can stick to a 500-800 calorie meal with similar food choices as the longer distance recommendation. If an athlete competing in this distance tolerates more food, exceeding 800 calories for the first meal should not have a negative impact.

After arriving at the race, sipping on a bottle of electrolyte plus carbohydrate beverage or having a banana at the ready before the swim is a good idea to ensure the carbohydrate stores are topped off.

Tip 63: Don't change a thing Part 2 — the race itself

The calorie needs vary widely depending on the distance of the race. As mentioned before, shorter distance races may not require any nutrition, while an Ironman requires a calculated plan. A few rules of thumb for in-race fueling apply across the board:

- The athlete should not try a product or amount of product that was not used in training.
- The athlete should not wait until he or she feels energy levels begin to dip.
- The athlete should be prepared to make changes on the fly if a bottle is dropped or if GI issues are present.

Nutritional strategies are specific to the individual. What works for one may result in vomiting for another. Some athletes like to keep liquid calories rolling all the way through the race and in training. Others tolerate a decent amount of solid food on the bike to fuel a fast run. The most important element of making race nutrition work on race day is practicing it in training. Training is a great place to make mistakes in all aspects of triathlon, and nutrition is no exception.

Tip 64: Race hydration

Much like race nutrition, race hydration begins in the days leading in. Sodium is an electrolyte crucial to muscle function and is at the heart of hydration. Using plain water when the sweat rate is high can result in a loss of sodium that is too large to overcome. Sipping on an electrolyte beverage or salting food in the days before a race can help an athlete stay hydrated. This becomes more essential for races that take place in hot climates in the middle of the summer.

Tip 65: Don't change a thing Part 3

Taking anything to the extreme in the days before a race is not advised. It can be easy to think that more sodium means better hydration or more water means better hydration, but there is a limit on what the body can process. A small increase in sodium and water intake is all that is needed.

Tip 66: During the race

A hydration strategy is highly individual, perhaps even more so than calorie intake. Everyone has a different sweat rate which is one of the main drivers of determining how much sodium to take in during a race. Furthermore, a sprint distance race may warrant no additional hydration. For longer races, a few rules of thumb can apply:

- The athlete should not try a new product or a new amount of product that was not used in training
- The athlete should investigate race venue weather conditions to determine if humidity will play a role in the overall race.
- If the race will be in a humid climate, the athlete would benefit from having a few training days in similar conditions to "test" hydration.
- The athlete should be aware of roughly how many hours the race will take. This greatly impacts the need for hydration products and the amount needing to be used.

Tip 67: Weight loss

Completing the training necessary to compete in a triathlon is a sound weight-loss strategy for an athlete looking to do so. In fact, many people sign up for a race as a means of staying committed to a weight loss goal. This is only one of the many health benefits associated with triathlon.

Weight loss can be taken to the extreme in the sport. A "lighter is better" mindset persists amongst higher-level athletes. While there is some merit to being at a specific race weight, it can be taken too far. There is some danger in becoming too lean. Bike power output decreases, recovery is impaired, and injuries can occur. If an athlete is keen on dropping weight for the sake of performance, it is best for that athlete to consult a dietician. The process must be done systematically because holding an ideal "race weight" is not feasible long term. An athlete accumulating significant training volume for a Half Ironman or Ironman would benefit from training a bit heavier. Training heavily is somewhat protective of the significant energy demands.

The well-fueled athlete will be the fastest, which does not always mean the lightest athlete. For an elite-level triathlete, this may be tough to understand because lighter weights typically manifest (initially) as better run performances. Better run performances are appealing to a motivated athlete; thus, there seems to be no deleterious impact. This performance gain is only sustainable if the athlete reaches this level with sustainable nutrition. Unsustainable nutrition, or under-fueling to achieve a lower weight, is not a recommended strategy to achieve peak performance. Again, the well-fueled athlete is the fastest.

Most athletes fall into a middle category, aiming for a good race performance while staying healthy. This can be achieved by sticking to a modest nutrition plan focused on nutrient-dense foods and fueling the training. "Race weight" usually takes care of itself when following the basics.

Tip 68: What's the deal with carbohydrates?

Carbohydrates can sometimes get a bad reputation in the mainstream media. Some claims posit that carbohydrates are bad for overall health, but much of the correlation between carbohydrates and declining health is in a sedentary population. The endurance athlete is far from sedentary.

In the endurance community, high fat/low carbohydrate nutrition gained popularity amongst the cohort of athletes targeting longer-distance races. The idea behind this type of diet is to teach the body to rely on fat as the primary fuel source. Remember, fat is essentially an unlimited fuel source, unlike carbohydrates. Some athletes have had undoubted success with this approach, but it is mostly limited to the longer races where relative intensity is low. Therefore, the casual endurance athlete looking to perform well in shorter, high-intensity races need not be afraid of carbohydrates. On the contrary, they are THE fuel that allows an athlete to achieve a high intensity and should be prioritized.

It should be mentioned that understanding how to use carbohydrates can improve an athlete's body composition and metabolism. Supplementing with the carbohydrate recommendations before, during, and immediately after training from **Tip 57** is what an athlete should aim for.

The time outside of training can be more difficult, and therefore, the meal immediately following a training session is important from a carbohydrate standpoint. Getting 100-150 grams of quality carbohydrates at this time can curb cravings later in the day. Athletes training one time per day can greatly benefit from reducing sugary and starchy carbohydrates in the evening. Emphasis on nutrient-dense food at this time can be great for improving body composition. Athletes training in the morning and in the evening, common amongst working adults, can be more flexible with spacing out the sugar and starch throughout the day to "fuel the day."

Feeling hungry can be common when training for a triathlon, but a few strategies can be effective in making sure hunger does not derail performance or derail diet:

- Prioritizing protein for feeling full (see **Tip 55**).
- Placing sugar in and around training and limiting it at other times of the day. The brain relates sugar and reward.
- Being diligent about intake during exercise to not reach levels of depletion.
- Monitoring intensity to ensure most training is performed aerobically, where fuel partitioning is driven by mostly fats.
- A well-fueled athlete stays on top of carbohydrate intake and sees its benefits in performance, recovery, and beyond!

Tip 69: Sports nutrition products

Products such as energy bars, gels, chews, and drink mixes are an important part of the overall nutrition plan for the athlete. Most of the products contain a hefty amount of carbohydrates in the form of pure cane sugar, maltodextrin, or some other variation of sugar. The case for using sports nutrition is that they are a user-friendly way to ingest carbohydrates during training or racing. Typically, brands have tailored the product to be fast digesting or easy on the stomach, and the serving sizes hover right around the 60-gram recommended threshold.

If used daily, bars, gels, chews, and drinks can be expensive. Substituting real food in daily training and saving sports nutrition for important sessions and races can be a good strategy to make nutrition more cost-effective. Some real food options for training can be:

- Dried fruit (dates, mangoes, apricots)
- Honey
- Maple syrup
- Bananas
- Fruit juices

An athlete must also become accustomed to a product that does not upset the stomach. Sugar can be hard on the gut, especially when ingested in large quantities. Training the gut is essential for longer distance athletes to find a product—real food or sports nutrition—

that works and is practical for race day. The only way to ensure smooth sailing on race day is to have practiced using a product multiple times in training. It would be foolish to expect to run fast without having done running in training. Nutrition is no different.

Tip 70: Sample nutrition plan

Navigating the grocery aisles to find the necessary fuel can be daunting for a first-time athlete. The easiest way to ensure staying on a solid diet plan is to develop a low standard deviation nutrition strategy. This means that there is a small rotation of foods the athlete eats throughout the week that is dependable. Large swings in the overall contents of a diet can make eating more difficult than it needs to be. When in doubt, keep it simple.

The following is a worked example of what a basic training day may look like for an amateur athlete looking to complete a sprint or Olympic distance. These are the most contested distances among triathletes. This plan assumes that most days feature two training sessions:

Wake up

16-24 oz (400-600 mL) water immediately

1/2 — ¾ cup of oatmeal with berries and honey

OR

Two pieces of whole grain toast w/choice of nut butter + a banana

1-hour swim session (no nutrition needed during, electrolyte beverage is optional)

Post-swim

1 cup Greek yogurt and whichever of the two above were not eaten before the swim

OR

3 whole eggs and whichever of the two above were not eaten before the swim

Morning snack

Whole piece of fruit and a handful of nuts

Whole piece of fruit and protein shake

Lunch

2-3 servings of vegetables + 1 cup potatoes or rice + 1 serving lean protein (chicken or fish)

16-24 oz (400-600 mL) water

Avocado or other healthy fat can be added if desired

Afternoon snack (optional if PM session is early afternoon)

Banana + scoop of nut butter

OR

1 name-brand energy bar (Larabar, ClifBar, etc.)

Afternoon training: 90 min bike ride with intensity + 20 min easy running off the bike

One large bottle of electrolyte beverage + 2 gels OR 2 scoops drink mix (taken on bike)

OR

One large bottle of electrolyte beverage + 4-6 pieces of dried fruit (taken on bike)

OR

One large bottle of electrolyte beverage + 3 fl. oz. (90 mL) maple syrup (taken on bike)

Post-training meal/dinner

Optional protein shake immediately following the session

2-3 servings of vegetables + 1-2 cups potatoes or rice + 1-1.5 servings lean protein (chicken, fish, lean beef)

Optional healthy fat source (avocado, olive oil, etc.)

Final snack (optional if dinner was late)

1 cup of berries + 2 squares dark chocolate

OR

1 cup berries + 1 cup cottage cheese/yogurt

OR

Another protein shake, if not taken after the workout.

This worked example is devoid of items such as packaged snacks and processed foods. Most days of training do not require them, but they are not entirely off-limits. A focus on whole foods, fueling during exercise when indicated, and protein intake will get an athlete most of the way there in terms of a sound nutritional base. The example above may drop the number of carbohydrates for dinner if the athlete has only trained once that day, reflecting the idea of keeping the carbs flowing primarily before, during, and immediately after training.

Chapter Review

This chapter covered the following:

- Basics of human metabolism
- Importance of nutrient density in the diet
- Fueling during exercise
- Weight loss and its place in sport
- A worked example of a daily nutrition plan

With a firm grasp on diet, an athlete can make significant gains without any extra training. Another area that can improve performance and requires no extra training is a focus on recovery. **Chapter 8** looks at the importance of rest and how an athlete can keep his or her body functioning at a high level.

Chapter 8: How to Recover

Tip 71: Rest is where growth happens

Stress + rest = growth. This is a simple formula used in the fitness and performance world that has considerable value. For a first-time athlete to compete and succeed in a triathlon, some training stress must be applied. The body needs to experience a new stimulus so that it can adapt, become strong, and handle the demands of a race. A progressive training program, like the one outlined in Chapter 6, is the best way to apply stress. Small and incremental additions are made to the program so as not to overwhelm the athlete. Remember, training is only a small part of life. Amateur athletes have other areas of life that are external stressors. Balance is key.

While the specifics of a training program are critical, the time spent away from training is where the gains are realized. This is referred to as the recovery part of training. An athlete can only train to the level of his or her recovery. It may seem simple to rest when needed, but the Type A triathlete personality is prone to going big on training at the expense of recovery. An athlete who waits until injury or illness takes them out of the game has waited too long to prioritize rest.

Rest has a few different connotations. Rest within a week, a season, before a race; all may look different. Rest also is not always passive. A solid training program often includes active rest days. The remainder of the chapter covers the different meanings of rest and how to make the most of the preparations for a triathlon.

Tip 72: Different rest periods

Rest within a day

Sufficient sleep and time to physically recharge comprise what is known as day-to-day recovery. Without sufficient recovery time, the training response to the planned program will be blunted, and the athlete will not achieve his or her full potential. Basic habits such as eating properly, managing stress, and getting to bed on time are the cornerstone of keeping a week rolling as planned.

Rest within a week

On a micro level, a basic week will feature easier days and harder days. The easier days are not full days off but are not intended to add more load. Adding load is saved for the harder training days. Modest amounts of aerobic training (Zone 1 and Zone 2) usually require little to no extended recovery time before an athlete can come back and do another session. The more intense sessions are usually best followed by an easy and low-intensity day to achieve the right amount of rest within a week.

Rest within a build-up

Some race distances require many months of slowly building up fitness. Pushing hard every week for 4-8 months is not a sustainable approach; thus, rest periods along the way are advised. A popular way to schedule a training program is to have 2-3 weeks of adding load through volume or intensity and then taking a week of reduced volume and intensity to consolidate the work. The process is repeated multiple times over in the Build phase and Race Specific phase until race day. The weeks of reduced work are not weeks of no training but allow the athlete to freshen up physically or tend to non-training life items more closely than during the "on" weeks. Inserting a small race or important workout at the end of a "down" week is common practice and a way to capitalize on feeling fresh.

Rest within a season

If the athlete is keen on making triathlon a year-round endeavor, a seasonal approach is helpful. It is essential that the athlete is not pushing all year long because holding top fitness year-round is not healthy or sustainable. At some point, the athlete must shed fatigue, whether heading into a race or in a proper offseason.

Racing multiple times a year can be a good safeguard against becoming too tired. This generally works well because taking 5-7 days of lower volume before and after a race can result in feeling fresh for another Build phase.

An offseason looks different for everyone. Some athletes prefer a few months of little activity and no structured training. Other athletes prefer working on a weakness for 4-6 weeks before starting a new Base phase. Regardless, every serious athlete can benefit from an extended downtime from rigorous training, and it need not include no physical activity. Spending some time in the gym getting strong, working on swimming technique, or exploring another sport entirely are some options for having a structured offseason.

Rest before the race

Freshness is a great feeling; every athlete chases feeling light and loose heading into a race. Most of the details on how to maximize the week heading into an event are covered in Chapter 6 under information on the Taper phase. Taking rest before a race ensures the athlete is firing on all cylinders and has consolidated the gains made during training in the months prior. It is common for the motivated, Type A personality to kick in during this time and push the athlete toward thinking he or she is losing fitness. Admittedly, some fitness is lost in a taper, but it is minimal in comparison to the performance benefit afforded by freshness. The work was done in the months before, not the week of.

Tip 73: Understanding fatigue

Fatigue is a tricky subject in triathlon. Too little, and the adaptations to training do not become realized. Too much and the adaptations to training do not become realized. As with most things in triathlon, balance is key. Some basic questions that an athlete can ask are helpful in striking the right balance. There is a time to push hard and a time to back off, and these times are unique to the individual.

Acute vs. chronic

There are two types of fatigue: acute and chronic.

Acute fatigue results after a hard training day or a series of hard training days. With proper rest and nutrition, the athlete can usually recover quickly from this type of fatigue, making gains in fitness along the way.

Chronic fatigue is a sense of tiredness or feeling flat in workouts for weeks or months in a row. This is usually a sign that the training program is not working for the athlete or that life outside of training is too stressful. If the athlete is experiencing any of the following:

- Poor sleep quality

- Low energy levels

- Major mood swings

- Impaired mental acuity

- Disinterest in training

- Sugar cravings

- Extreme weight loss

It is worth looking at the pillars of recovery—Sleep, Nutrition, Training Load—and consulting with the coach (it may be the athlete himself) to adjust the plan. Backing off before it is too late can save an athlete from ruin. These situations sound extreme but are common among triathletes.

What does feeling exceptional feel like?

One of the questions an athlete can ask is, "how does exceptional feel?" If the athlete never feels exceptional at some point during the year or the build-up to a race, that is a cause for concern. Balancing weeks of increased volume or intensity followed by a week of rest serves as a frequent reminder of what feeling great is like. The athlete should never be so far in the hole that he or she forgets the sensation of being at his or her best.

Does life permit adding more training load?

Acute fatigue can turn into chronic fatigue in a hurry when an athlete adds intensity during a period of stressful work life or family life. Everything that is added has a cost, and this cost must always be accounted for. Overloading on life and training does not work. Make sure life circumstances permit increases in training. If they do not, sticking to a program like the 3x3 protocol encourages getting something done each day without reaching the hand too far in the cookie jar.

Does the training data support doing more or doing less?

Keeping a training log comes in handy to answer this question. Past history is a great way to inform future decisions. If the athlete is considering adding an element to training that is radically different than anything done in the past, either tread lightly or do not engage at all. This question is also relevant for an athlete who may be struggling with executing a program with consistency. A string of unimpressive and consistent workouts does far more for the athlete than one stellar workout. Accumulated work is a key element of preparing for a triathlon.

Tip 74: Sleep

Sleep is a free and legal performance enhancer. Cognitive function, physical output, and overall mood improve with sufficient sleep. On top of the demand of triathlon training, most amateur athletes are balancing a job, a family, or both, and operating well in all of those spaces requires physical and mental health.

Recommendations for sleep in adults is between 7-9 hours. Ideally, an athlete will want to aim for the high end of the range to consolidate the gains of training, but a busy lifestyle may not permit that much sleep. There are a few strategies worth employing if an athlete finds it difficult to get enough sleep.

Tip 75: *Firm to bed/wake time*

One way to make less sleep effective is to maintain consistency. Less sleep, in this case, means on the lower end of 7-9 hours. Keeping a set bedtime and wake-up time pays off over time. Perhaps the athlete is consistently logging 7 hours of sleep per night. This is far better than a few nights of 4 hours, a night of 8 hours, a night of 6 hours, and so on. It may require getting other areas of life in order, but the payoff of consistency is well worth it.

Tip 76: *Capitalize on the time spent in bed*

Cleaning up the sleep environment is an effective strategy for falling asleep and staying asleep. Limiting cell phone use, limiting caffeine consumption, and keeping the room dark and cool are worthy considerations for making the most of the time spent in bed.

Tip 77: *Prioritize*

If the athlete has been low on sleep for a few days and has an important training day coming up, it is worth placing emphasis on sleep rather than getting the session done. Sleeping more and opting for an easy day of training can help the body be prepared for doing the planned hard or long session the next day if the schedule allows it. If the training has been consistently "good" in the weeks prior, one missed or reprogrammed workout when it is *really* needed will not ruin progress. In fact, it may accelerate progress! Nothing beats staying healthy.

Tip 78: The "recovery workout" and active recovery

The term recovery workout may seem counterintuitive. "Workout" implies working hard and breaking a sweat, but that is not always the case. Active recovery can be an essential component of an athlete's program when it is done correctly.

The recovery workout is intended to feel too easy. Many new athletes may be surprised that a short 15-20 minutes of walking after a meal can be labeled as active recovery. Getting the blood flowing and staying loose is the aim. Active recovery does not necessarily improve performance, but it can help the athlete prepare for the bigger sessions that may be coming or loosen up after a hard training day.

In a training context, a recovery session may be warranted if the athlete is overly stressed with outside events (family, work, etc.). Instead of missing a day completely, active recovery can maintain the habit of consistency.

Two rules exist with active recovery:

- Short duration
- Low (ridiculously low) in intensity
- Some examples for each of the three disciplines may include:
- Swim: 15-20 min straight swim with a pull buoy. Think "floating"
- Bike: 30-60 minutes at Zone 1 intensity or below. Think "Zone 0"
- Run: 15-30 minutes at Zone 1 intensity or below. Think "light on feet"

If the athlete is pressed for time during the week, the emphasis should be on completing the plan before adding in specific active recovery. Nonspecific active recovery can be inserted at any time, such as walking after a meal or during the workday.

Tip 79: Sore or injured?

There will be times throughout a training program when the athlete's body is *feeling* it. This is a natural byproduct of being tired, but it is essential that the athlete knows the distinction between soreness and an injury.

Soreness

Being sore typically manifests as a dull ache and heaviness in the muscles. The athlete may feel slow and sluggish to start a workout, but symptoms typically may clear by the end of a low-intensity session. Soreness can last a few days and generally will not inhibit the athlete from performing training. However, prolonged soreness or stiffness should be a red flag as it may indicate a shortcoming of sleep, poor diet, or an ineffective training program.

Injury

Injuries are all too common in triathlon and are usually present because of doing too much too soon or because of a traumatic occurrence, i.e., a bike crash. The traumatic variety is apparent, and the athlete usually knows the severity.

A nagging pain in the knee from repetitive running, for example, might not follow that same path. A determined athlete wants to complete the training and sometimes may train through injury. This is not always advised and can lead to greater setbacks in the buildup to a race.

Tip 80: Pain as a guide for injuries

Fortunately, most chronic injuries, such as an inflamed tendon, can be managed with little to no derailment of the training program. The simple guide below can help an athlete navigate pain. In this case, an athlete can continue activity at an easier intensity than planned if:

- Pain level does not exceed 5/10 during training
- Pain level resides at 0-3/10 after
- Swimming, cycling, and running mechanics are not altered by pain
- Pain is not progressing in severity week to week

In cases of severe pain (>6/10), the athlete should refrain from training and either rest for a few days while monitoring symptoms or consult a physio. After gathering information on the source of the injury, it is worth examining the training program or life outside of training to identify where the training load may have been too extreme. Some chronic injuries are a result of poor equipment or technique, but most athletes fall victim to injury due to training too much or too hard.

Tip 81: *Running as the injury culprit*

Running can be hard on an athlete's legs. Swimming and cycling are relatively low impact and feature injuries less frequently than running. One benefit triathlon provides over pure run training is that all three sports can complement one another. When developing a self-coached or coached program, airing on the side of light running volume is a smart strategy for a beginner in triathlon. The bike can be a powerful tool for keeping the legs strong and the fitness high without pounding out running miles that the athlete is not prepared for.

Not only will the athlete improve his or her chances of avoiding any injury hiccups when preparing for the first race, but he or she will also improve the chances of developing long term for future races.

Tip 82: *Recovery products + tools*

No amount of fancy massage therapy or vitamin supplements can replace the need for sleep, proper diet, and controlled training. It is easy to get caught up in the marketing around recovery products that guarantee faster recovery or improved performance. This does not mean that dietary supplements, massage guns/therapy, or ice baths are useless, but these products should be considered a bonus.

Massage guns and massage therapy

Muscles will get sore during training. It is a fact of life. Recent advances in technology have made massage guns available to the everyday consumer and can help target particularly bothersome sore spots to provide relief. Some athletes swear by them or swear by seeing a masseuse, but it should be noted that a massage gun or an appointment with a masseuse is expensive. The athlete must budget for this if he or she is to make it part of the normal recovery routine.

Dietary supplements

On the nutritional front, supplements can be a tricky arena to navigate. Not only do most have limited evidence for being effective, but some can be deleterious to an athlete's performance. Therefore, before starting any supplementation, an athlete may want to consult a doctor to find out more details related to the pros and cons.

One tried, and true supplement used widely in the endurance world is caffeine. There is no question that caffeinated beverages or other mediums enhance performance by ramping up the nervous system, thereby increasing feelings of alertness. Many sports nutrition products have combined simple sugar and caffeine for a double whammy of feeling energized. The caveat with caffeine is that too much can make one feel sick or anxious, and taking it too close to bedtime can disrupt sleep. Sleep is the most potent supplement on the market, and it is best to protect sleep quality at all costs.

Moreover, dietary supplements also harness a monetary cost, and an athlete needs to budget for it if he or she is looking to use a product consistently.

Stretching and mobility

A recovery tool with a high return on investment is having a stretching or mobility routine. Tight muscles and immobile joints can lead to injury or discomfort during training. A simple 10-minute routine at night or in the morning is plenty. Areas that commonly become tight or sore in triathlon are the hips, ankles, hamstrings, and sometimes shoulders. There are no special stretches that every athlete should be doing. The mobility routine is intended to make the athlete feel "good" or feel "loose," and this can be achieved in a variety of ways. Explore how the body moves.

Mental rest

Training requires intense mental focus at times, and gathering the motivation to execute the planned program consistently can be difficult. Periods of mental rest where the athlete unplugs from athletic life are important for maintaining a fresh and positive mindset. Being able to recharge by reading a book, hanging out with friends, or exploring a hobby are overlooked recovery tools that can have a material impact on athletic success.

Tip 83: Advanced recovery tracking

A first-time triathlete can go a long way in the sport by relying on subjective metrics to guide recovery. Subjective measures are based on the opinions of the athlete toward how he or she feels. These items may include:

- Feeling energized/tired
- Soreness level
- Mood
- Sense of enjoyment/dread during training
- Positive/negative outlook toward training/work/life balance

However, there is some use for objective metrics to track recovery. Objective measures are information about the physiological state of the athlete based on data. An athlete should only dive into objective metrics if he or she understands the meaning of what they can provide. In many cases, they can add confusion for the beginner athlete. These items include:

- Monitoring resting heart rate
- Monitoring heart rate response
- Monitoring heart rate variability HRV
- Monitoring training load using a training software

Heart rate information

The heart can be a powerful source of information for how an athlete is recovering.

A simple morning resting heart rate measurement is a way to assess fatigue or the potential onset of illness. After a typical range has been established from a few measurements, a value higher than a normal range is a caution signal. On the other hand, a consistent morning value or even one that decreases over time can be indicative of coping well with training and gaining fitness.

Furthermore, assessing the heart rate response to exercise can add context to the resting heart rate.

A high resting value coupled with difficulty raising heart rate during exercise can be the body's way of putting the brakes on higher-intensity exercise. This is known as suppression.

A high resting value coupled with an abnormally high heart rate during exercise can be indicative of illness. Usually, an athlete will feel other symptoms if the heart rate is out of control at rest and in training.

In either case above, if something looks abnormal, it is best that the athlete relies on subjective measures to help decide how to proceed. Opting for a low-intensity day or no training at all can be a safe bet.

An even deeper level of analysis is featured in a technology known as heart rate variability (HRV). It is a topic still developing in the endurance sports realm, but the gist of its use case in sports is that it can give the athlete or coach of the athlete a picture of how the body is responding to stress. The technology monitors the time between beats of the heart. Variation in these beats usually means that the body is in a restful and relaxed state. The lack of variation suggests the opposite.

There are many apps on the market, such as HRV4Training, that provide meaning to a daily measurement to help guide training. As with resting heart rate, a range is set, and long-term trends are what are most important. HRV is an advanced topic, and the first-time triathlete should not be concerned with using it if he or she does not understand the data.

Training software — load management

Chapter 3 mentioned a software called TrainingPeaks that can help an athlete track training load. Other apps such as Garmin Connect, Today's Plan, and more work similarly. Each activity is assigned a particular stress score based on how intense it was, and an overall stress load for a week, month, or year is developed. While not a perfect indicator of load, it can be helpful in conjunction with other measures to illustrate how a plan is working and how best to move forward.

Like the other objective measures, this is an advanced topic commonly used by athletes who have been competing for multiple years. Some coaches start first-time triathletes on plans that use training software, but it is not a necessary component to training, competing, and succeeding in a triathlon.

Chapter Review

This chapter covered the following:

- The meaning of rest and its many connotations
- Understanding fatigue
- Importance of sleep
- Active recovery

- Essential tools for recovery
- Advanced strategies for tracking recovery

Training, eating, and recovering are all important to triathlon, but there are some unexpected pieces of the puzzle that a first-time athlete must know. **Chapter 9** covers the things nobody may tell an athlete before the first race or before starting an arduous training plan.

Chapter 9: What They Don't Tell You Before Training for and Racing in Triathlons

Tip 84: *Know the rules of the race*

Nearly every race has the rules published on the website from which an athlete will sign up. It is recommended to read these rules even if most of the rules seem like common sense, i.e., wearing a helmet on a bike. Other rules, such as drafting behind other riders during the bike, can be more nuanced. One race may require 20 feet between bikes, while other races may require 60 feet. It simply depends. There are officials at races, and rules are enforced. An athlete should do his or her due diligence to read the rulebook.

Tip 85: *Transitions*

The time between the swim and the bike, and the bike and the run, are known as the transition period. Transition can be a tricky part of the race to navigate because it is a balance between working quickly and not forgetting essential gear. Even experienced athletes can struggle with transition.

The best way to improve efficiency in transition is to practice. It is a part of the race and deserves attention.

The designated transition area is set up near the swim, bike, and run course but can sometimes require a short run from the swim course to the transition area. Inside are rows of metal racks from which an athlete hangs the bike and lays out necessary gear. Each race has a slightly different setup, but the basic design is consistent among all races.

Tip 86: Swim to bike

Completing a swim-bike brick workout is difficult to organize logistically. Most athletes never get this experience in training and learn through doing multiple races as opposed to practicing. The part of the swim-bike transition that can trip athletes up is the case of a wetsuit swim. Taking off a wetsuit is a process that should be practiced before a race. The suits are tight, making removal a hassle if the athlete has not practiced. A simple workflow for stripping off a wetsuit in a timely fashion is as follows:

1. Find the zipper cord and unzip the suit while running to the bike

2. Pull the suit off one shoulder, then the other shoulder

3. Slide the suit down to the feet

4. Remove one leg

5. Use the removed leg to step on the suit for ease of removing the other leg

6. Store the wetsuit within the transition slot chosen. Don't leave it out in the open!

After removing the wetsuit, it is time to put on gear for the bike. A helmet is always required for races, so it is a good idea to put this on immediately. Next, the athlete must get the bike to the designated "mount line" before starting to ride the bike. There are a few options for navigating this process.

- Pick up bike shoes, run with them in hand, put them on at the mount line, and start riding
- Run with bike shoes on to mount line (not recommended), start riding
- Use tennis shoes and not bike cleats (common for a beginner)
- Learn a flying mount (advanced skill)

A flying mount is a time-saving strategy where the bike shoes are clipped into the pedals before the race. The athlete runs with the bike to the mount line and jumps on the bike. The first few pedal strokes are done with the feet on top of the shoes, and once momentum is gained from pedaling, the athlete coasts and inserts feet into the shoes. This strategy is used by many experienced triathletes and requires practice to avoid crashing the bike.

The best swim-bike transition will result from the following:

- Working quickly and calmly. Rushing makes the athlete prone to error.
- Doing only what has been practiced, i.e., do not try a flying mount without practicing

Tip 87: Bike to run

The easier transition to practice in training is the bike-run. This can be accomplished by setting out running shoes before a bike training session and seeing how fast one can hop off the bike and change into running shoes.

Dismount

There is a mount line when starting the bike portion and a dismount line at the end. It is crucial that the athlete is off of the bike ahead of this line to avoid a penalty. Like the swim-bike transition, there are a few ways to navigate this:

- Stop the bike, unclip shoes, remove shoes, and run with the bike to the transition spot
- Stop the bike, unclip shoes, and run with bike shoes on to transition spot (not recommended)
- If using tennis shoes: Stop the bike, run to the transition spot
- Learn a flying dismount (advanced skill)

The flying dismount involves removing the feet from the shoes and swinging a leg over the seat while still moving. The athlete then stops the bike just before the dismount line and begins running to the transition spot.

Socks?

Many athletes do not wear socks on the bike in the interest of time and may also forgo socks for the run. However, if the athlete is unsure how his or her feet respond to running sockless in running shoes, take a few extra seconds to throw on socks. Getting a blister mid-run, especially in longer distances, can be painful and disruptive to an athlete's performance.

Shoes

If using bike shoes, the athlete will need to switch to running shoes before heading out on the course. To save time, investing in some quick laces or elastic laces can be helpful for slipping shoes on.

Race number

Nearly every race requires the athlete to wear a designated race number provided by the race during the run. This is usually provided in the form of a paper bib. The easiest way to attach this is to a shirt or shorts that will be worn in the race via pins. However, not every athlete will be wearing a shirt or shorts in the race. Some may have a triathlon suit. In this case, purchasing a race belt can be a good idea. Race belts allow the race bib to be attached, and some belts are designed to carry small nutrition items like gels too.

Simple bike-run workflow

While every athlete has his or her own preferences for what to wear during the run, a basic workflow for navigating the bike-run transition is as follows:

- Dismount bike
- Run to transition spot and rack bike
- Remove helmet
- Socks optional; running shoes not optional!
- Put on race number (various ways)

- Get out on the course, quick!
- Like with the swim-bike, the fastest transition in the bike-run will result from:
- Working quickly and calmly. Rushing makes the athlete prone to error.
- Doing only what has been practiced, i.e., do not try a flying dismount without practicing

Tip 88: Setting up T1/T2

The first and second transitions are referred to as T1 and T2. Setting up the area before the race begins is an easy way to avoid errors during the race.

Timing chip + body marking

Before entering the transition area, the athlete will receive a timing chip to record the overall time on the day for results purposes. The chip is usually attached to the ankle, and it is essential that it is secure. Make this a priority. A race volunteer will also need to write the designated race number on the arm and leg to account for possible loss of the timing chip and for identification on the race course.

The transition spot

Selecting a transition spot comes down to athlete preference. For a beginner, it is hard to go wrong with choosing a spot. Once at the spot, putting down a towel or mat is a good idea to keep everything dry and in one spot. Next, racking the bike on the provided metal rack should be done. Any necessary hydration or nutrition bottles should be placed on the bike at this time. The race may also provide additional race number stickers to be put on the helmet or the bike. Do this now.

Under the bike, the athlete can begin to lay out the run shoes, socks, race bib, and bike helmet on the towel or mat that was put down. If there is any nutrition or special hydration for the run, it should be placed out at this time.

The final step is to grab the swim cap, goggles, and wetsuit (if indicated) and head down to the water to either do a swim warmup or survey the course from on land. Typically the transition area closes 15-20 minutes before the start of the race, so it is best to get in, get set up, and get out with plenty of time to spare.

Tip 89: Aid stations

An aspect of a race that an athlete may not experience until race day is the aid stations on the course. Most offer water, some form of electrolyte beverage, and some solid food or gels. Aid can be found every mile or half a mile during the run portion. Longer races will have aid stations on the bike. As with any of the nutrition planning covered in Chapter 7, if the athlete is not taking plain water, he or she must be familiar with the products taken from the aid station. Races will often advertise what products will be available, so reading that information beforehand can be helpful for beginning to train with similar items.

Another common issue beginner athletes face is learning to take in liquids while running. One of the most tried and true strategies is to slow down or walk through the aid station to ensure the liquid gets down. In short sprint races, aid stations may be skipped entirely, but walking a few aid stations in an Ironman is well worth the short hiatus in running.

Finally, aid stations may also have first-aid equipment on hand. Accidents happen in races, and it is good to have peace of mind knowing that safeguards have been put in place to get an athlete proper care if an unlikely injury or emergency were to happen.

Tip 90: Stay for awards and post-race festivities

Whether the athlete is the grand champion on the day or crossing the line amongst the pack, attending the award ceremony can be an enlightening experience. For a first-time athlete, seeing the community come together to honor the top performers in each age group is great motivation to continue to do more racing.

Many races also have post-race festivities at the finish line, such as raffle events, food trucks, and social time with other participants. There is tremendous value in sticking around and talking to other participants to learn indifferent perspectives, be a part of the community, and get a full experience.

Tip 91: Open water swimming

Chapter 4 explained how it is critical for an athlete to practice swimming in open water (lake or ocean) before race day. Murky water, waves, and cold water temperatures can be off-putting to some. Another feature of open water swimming in a race setting is swimming in a crowd of people. Races may have a mass start of thousands of athletes at once, and getting trampled is a possibility. Furthermore, an athlete who is fearful of swimming around a crowd of people is likely to panic in the water, which is not a recipe for enjoyment during a triathlon.

Some safeguards have been put into place to help novice swimmers feel more comfortable during the swim. "Swim waves" are common in races, so athletes choose a group based on pace. Waves go off in a staggered start fashion, with the slowest group last to ensure faster swimmers are not impeding on the slower swimmers.

The wave design still does not solve the fear of swimming in a group, but it makes the race start less hectic and keeps similar-speed athletes together; thus, the swim is less of a "free for all" for the novice athlete.

Tip 92: The dreaded "bonk"

Chapter 7 covered the importance of fueling before and during a race. Failure to do so can result in what is known as a "bonk" or hitting the wall. However, fueling properly does not guarantee that the athlete will not run out of energy during a race.

Intensity level is an often-overlooked contributor to fading during the race. It is surprisingly easy to overstep physical limits when the motivation is high and adrenaline is pumping early in a race. On the other hand, the athlete can do everything right on the nutrition front and still fall apart due to burning too many matches at the beginning of the race. No amount of sugar can make up for operating at an intensity that the athlete did not account for in training. Therefore, a nutrition plan and a pacing plan are equally important.

Tip 93: Mental strength

An athlete can have elite-level physical fitness, but without a strong mind, completing a triathlon will be difficult. Mental strength has a variety of meanings, but in the context of triathlon, mindset is one of the most important components.

Be positive

Having a positive attitude toward training is essential. When developing a program, most of the training should be enjoyable. Even the hard sessions should elicit a sense of accomplishment when complete. If the athlete is frequently feeling negative about working toward the goal of competing and succeeding in a race, then it is worth examining the program as a whole and reminding oneself of the core reason for wanting to sign up.

Detaching from the training and taking on a wide-lensed view can provide a sense of clarity. The athlete is far more than a race performance. This is not to say that the primary motivation cannot be racing fast, but a large majority of the triathlon community is in the sport for physical health, self-efficacy, and a reason to join a supportive community. Unfortunately, those who aim to compete at a high level can sometimes lose sight of this.

The athlete is part of a community who is engaging in a healthy and fun activity. That in itself is something to be positive about.

It is a process

No triathlete got his or her first race right on the first try. Mistakes will be made and should not be a source of discouragement. Being in a rush to achieve the goal of being ready for a race can leave an athlete prone to more mistakes than if he or she took the necessary time to develop. Development also does not always refer to physical attributes. Having the right attitude requires development too.

A foolproof training program does not exist. Life will get in the way, motivation will wane at times, and setbacks will occur. However, the athlete who understands the process embraces these obstacles and gains perspective from them. Success does not come from perfection but rather from adapting to imperfection.

It is not only a sport

Enduring a physical and mental challenge like a triathlon is an excellent proxy for other areas of life. The training, time management, sacrifices, and sense of accomplishment are informative of how an athlete can become impervious to any challenge that comes his or her way. In fact, many triathletes find that the lifestyle fits in with a high-achieving lifestyle in work, family, or finance.

Tip 94: Motivation

Being motivated every day for the months leading into a race is unrealistic. It is easy to assume, based on the triathlete Type A stereotype, that all triathletes are always getting after it in training, but that is not the case. Each athlete has his or her periods of low motivation, and it is important to know that it is part of the process. If motivation is low, there are some tips to rekindle the fire.

Training with friends

A large portion of the training in triathlon is slow, steady, and boring, but this is a perfect opportunity to call up some friends. "Talking pace" is a cue used in Chapter 5 to describe appropriately easy training. Running or cycling in a group can be a great time to chat and catch up with friends while making the training time fly by. Calling up a buddy can provide accountability for getting the planned work accomplished.

Group work is popular for the hard training days as well. Shared hardship in the form of exercise is a powerful motivator as it gives that extra push to conquer the workout. A quick search online usually returns results of local swim, bike, or run groups that an athlete can join to serve this purpose.

Sign up for a small race

With a months-long training plan, it can be hard to see the light at the end of the tunnel. However, inserting a small race on the calendar can be all that is needed to keep the fire burning hot. These races do not need to be a peak focus and should be focused on fun. Entering a local 5K run or signing up for an open water 500-meter swim are examples. Not only can this improve motivation to keep training, but it can also give valuable data for assessing progress toward the bigger goal of doing a triathlon.

Switch up the music

It may seem silly, but introducing new music to the workout playlist can be helpful for putting some pep in the step. Music is a powerful medium during exercise and has been shown to decrease the sensation of pain in a hard workout. There is reason to assume it can also improve motivation through a similar mechanism, so turn up the beat!

Watch the pros

Each year, the Ironman World Championship is broadcast on television and can be a great source of inspiration. Watching the world's best duel it out on an iconic race course is enough to give an athlete a much-needed lift in training. Ironman is not the only televised triathlon, but it is the most well-known for the average fan. There is a lot to be learned from professionals.

Embrace

The low motivation days are part of the process, as long as the motivation is not constantly absent; a few tough days here and there are considered normal. Some of these days, the best option is to embrace the feeling and get the work done. Doing the work is not glamorous but has a major return on investment in the race and on creating momentum. Remember the low motivation days when striding across the finish line after months of hard work. Choosing the hard right over the easy wrong contributed to this successful day at the race.

Tip 95: Becoming a lifer

Anyone can become a triathlete at any time. This does not mean it is easy, but it does mean that nobody should shy away from triathlon because it seems too hard. Often, athletes cross the finish line of his or her first race and have already decided to race again in the future. There is something powerful about learning and growing in the training process that makes the sport addictive. Attend any local race, and there are likely to be a few 70+ year-olds out on the course who have been participating for years purely out of enjoyment.

There are a variety of distances that can be done at a variety of speeds. There is something for everyone, and it is why, with the right approach, triathlon can be a sustainable hobby for life.

Tip 96: New perspectives

One of the best parts about training and competing in a triathlon is the perception of doing difficult tasks. An athlete can gain a new perspective on what "hard" truly means, and this perspective can be informative in tackling other challenges in life. The sport is one of the best teachers of life's lessons and as much a medium for physical health as it is for self-improvement.

Chapter Review

This chapter covered the following:

- Knowing the race rules
- Mastering transitions
- Getting comfortable in open water
- Building mental strength
- Keeping motivated
- Gaining a new perspective on hard tasks

The longest distance race in the sport, Ironman, draws a lot of attention because of its length and difficulty. While this book will not cover a full "how to" for an Ironman, some important themes to consider when trying the distance are covered in **Chapter 10.**

Chapter 10: The Ironman

Ironman is an advanced topic that warrants its own book entirely. The distance, training, and life demands are a significant level up from more modest sprint, Olympic, or Half Ironman distance races. However, that does not mean that Ironman is unpopular. In fact, it is one of the more popular race distances, and thousands of people each year decide to commit to the challenge. This chapter touches less on the "how to" of Ironman and more on the important things to consider before signing up.

Tip 97: *Understand the demand of the race itself*

One part of Ironman that is difficult for people to grasp is how demanding the race is. At face value, it is a 2.4 mile (3.8 km) swim, 112 mile (180 km) bike, and 26.2 mile (42 km) run. What does that really entail?

It entails moving for many hours. The fastest Ironman athletes finish in the range of 7-9 hours which is a long time for a novice to conceptualize. The first-time Ironman finisher crosses the line in double the time, 14-17 hours.

Before deciding to do an Ironman, get comfortable with the idea of moving for the better portion of a day. The distance is not to be underestimated, and a backward planning approach can work in an athlete's favor.

How long will this take? 15 hours? Alright, now let's plan training around working at a 15-hour pace, not a 10-hour pace.

Tip 98: *Understand the demand for the training*

Becoming fit enough to complete an Ironman requires a substantial amount of training. There is no minimum number of hours or magic number of hours to complete, but amateur athletes are logging 12, 15, and 20-hour weeks of training for months before the event.

The training is also not a walk in the park. 5-hour bike rides, 2-hour runs, and long swims are major features in the training diet. Before deciding to do an Ironman, an athlete must ask whether he or she is willing to accumulate the time necessary to become an Ironman.

Tip 99: Understand the demand in everyday life

An amateur working triathlete will need to make some sacrifices to accumulate those hours. Family members need to be in support of the journey, work life needs to be in order, and the athlete needs to have the time to dedicate to training. Burning down family and work life in pursuit of completing an Ironman is not advised.

This is not to say that many hardworking parents are not competing in Ironman. They are! In fact, it is a popular sport amongst mothers and fathers. The key is to have buy-in from the support system, whether that is friends or family, and to get comfortable with making tough choices on occasion. That 5-hour ride may need to be postponed, or it may mean missing a child's soccer game on the weekend to get it done. It may not even happen at all, and it is important to remember that perfect race preparation is not needed to become an Ironman.

Tip 100: Experience level

Athletic experience greatly determines the time course it will take for an athlete to accumulate the hours needed to complete an Ironman. For example, someone just getting into exercise may require years of basic training, while a former college athlete may be only a few months from Ironman fitness.

The best advice is to experiment with shorter distance racing before making any plans for an Ironman. If an Olympic distance is a struggle, there is still some athletic development needing to be done. Rushing the process can make Ironman preparation unenjoyable and decrease the chances of success.

Another sound piece of advice is to employ a coach. The shorter races are more straightforward in terms of showing up and getting across the line. Ironman is a new breed of race, and a coach with experience in the sport can develop a plan that keeps an athlete on track for the big day.

No matter an athlete's experience level, Ironman is an achievable goal. The achievement will be realized when the athlete gives the process time to unfold, however long that may be.

Tip 101: Finances

Ironman is an investment. Race sign-up, gear, coaching, traveling, and time off work all require a financial contribution. An athlete must develop a budget to avoid breaking the bank in the process of preparing for an Ironman. The following list of the most important items to budget for considers necessity and increasing chances at racing success.

- Triathlon bike ~$2,000-6,000
- GPS watch ~$100-300
- Race entry ~$500
- Travel to race if not local ~variable $
- Coaching fees (highly recommended) ~variable $ per month
- Pool membership ~$20-100 per month
- Grocery bill ~variable $

The investment is not to be looked down upon. Completing an Ironman is an accomplishment well worth the time and financial commitment. Moreover, the race distance can provide lessons in overcoming hardship that a $30 self-help book cannot.

Chapter Review

This chapter covered the following:

- The demands of Ironman
- Importance of a support system
- The influence of experience level on how long it will take to be ready
- The financial side of racing an Ironman

The final chapter, **Chapter 11**, serves as a key workout index where the athlete can gain inspiration for how to develop a custom training program.

Chapter 11: The Ultimate Workout Index

The final chapter of this book serves as a workout library from which an athlete can pull key workouts for sprint and Olympic distance training. All of the workouts follow the basic principles from Chapters 5 and 6, such as intensity control, proper warmup/cooldown, and specificity to race demands. Each distance has two workouts per discipline focused on different elements of training. The workouts are designed to be high-intensity sessions that should be included in a training plan that prioritizes easy Zone 1 and 2 volumes. Workout durations may vary based on the athlete's ability level and experience.

Tip 102: Sprint distance training

Swim workouts

Workout 1

<u>Warmup</u>

400 warmup

300 pulling

12x25 1 fast 1 easy :20 rest

<u>Main set</u>

18x100

3 steady :10 rest

2 strong :20 rest

1 fast :30 rest

Repeat x3

<u>Technique set</u>

75

50

25

50

75

Repeat X2

*All with 10 rest

*All easy with perfect technique

Workout 2

<u>Warmup</u>

500 warmup

300 pulling

100 build up to fast

<u>Main set</u>

200 steady :10 seconds rest

6x50 fast :30 seconds rest between each

200 steady :10 seconds rest

6x50 fast :30 seconds rest between each

200 steady

*Fast in this set is the best possible pace without falling apart

<u>Technique set</u>

3x100 breathing pattern every 3 strokes

150 pulling

3x100 breathing pattern every 5 strokes

*All of the swimming in this set is relaxed and focused on flow

Bike workouts

Workout 1

15-20 min warmup
*Start easy and increase to steady

10-15x 1 min hard 1 min easy
*Athlete chooses the number of rounds that are appropriate

15 min steady Zone 2 to finish
*steady Zone 2 should be manageable if the 1-minute efforts were paced correctly!

Workout 2

10 minutes Zone 1
10 minutes low Zone 2
10 minutes high Zone 2

8x 2 min hard Zone 5 effort/heart rate/power + 2 min easy Zone 1
*Work to be consistent across all 8 rounds! Start conservative.

10 min Zone 1 cooldown

Run workouts

Workout 1

15-20 min warmup
*Start easy and increase to steady
*Athlete choice of throwing in strides, run drills, quick sprints if familiar with these

6x400 meters on track/200 meters jog

*goal 5K race pace

*focus on form and consistent times

15 min jog cooldown

Workout 2

15-20 min warmup

*Start easy and increase to steady

*Athlete choice of throwing in strides, run drills, quick sprints if familiar with these

800 meters + 200 jog

600 meters + 200 jog

400 meters + 200 jog

400 meters + 200 jog

600 meters + 200 jog

800 meters + 200 jog

*goal 5K race pace

*focus on form and consistent times

15 min jog cooldown

Tip 103: Olympic distance training
Swim workouts
Workout 1

<u>Warmup</u>

400 warmup rest :30 seconds

3x100 pulling rest :10 between each
200 build rest :30 seconds
4x25 fast rest :20 between each
100 easy

Main set

50 max effort! rest :10 seconds
1x150 Zone 4 effort/pace rest :15 seconds
1x100 Zone 4 effort/pace rest :15 seconds
1x150 Zone 4 effort/pace rest :15 seconds
1x100 Zone 4 effort/pace rest :15 seconds
1x100 easy! rest 1 minute
repeat x3
*Important to carefully pace the first round to avoid sacrificing round 3
*The workout is designed to simulate a fast start of a race and then settling into a pace

200 easy cooldown

Workout 2

Warmup

400 swim :30 seconds rest
400 swim alternating breathing every 3 strokes + every 5 strokes by 50, :30 seconds rest
2x200 build up to strong :30 seconds rest between each
4x25 fast :15 rest between each

Main set

4x150 :20 rest between each, steady and strong pace

8x50 Zone 4 effort/pace :10 rest between each

2x300 :20 rest between each, steady and strong pace

8x50 Zone 4 effort/pace :10 rest between each

200 easy cooldown

Bike workouts

Workout 1

15-20 min warmup

*Start easy and increase to steady

5x6 minutes Zone 4 effort, heart rate, or power

*2 min recovery between each repetition

Finish with 20 minutes of steady Zone 2 riding

*steady Zone 2 should be manageable if the 6-minute efforts were paced correctly!

Workout 2

15-20 min warmup

*Start easy and increase to steady

6x

5 minutes Zone 4 effort, heart rate, power

5 minutes Zone 2 effort, heart rate, power

*An hour of consistent work

*Learning to recover at an intensity higher than Zone 1 with the Zone 2 portions

5 minutes cooldown

Run workouts
Workout 1
15-20 min warmup

*Start easy and increase to steady

*Athlete choice of throwing in strides, run drills, quick sprints if familiar with these

6x800 meters on track/200 meters jog

*Goal 10K pace for the 800 meters

*Focus on progressing throughout making the last one or two the strongest

15 minutes cooldown jog

Workout 2
15-20 min warmup

*Start easy and increase to steady

*Athlete choice of throwing in strides, run drills, quick sprints if familiar with these

3x1600 meters (1 mile) on track/400 meters jog

*Start a few seconds slower than 10K race pace

*Finish a few seconds under 10K race pace

4x 30 seconds hill sprints

*Focused on being quick and powerful

10 minutes cooldown jog

Chapter Review

This chapter covered:

- Workout ideas for sprint distance training programs
- Workout ideas for Olympic distance training programs

What a blast it has been to learn about the sport of triathlon! From the history to the training to the nuances of race day, you, the athlete, have covered it all. Sticking to the basics and remembering to have fun are two ways to take the tips learned in this book and put them into action. A careful plan executed with a hint of positivity is sure to propel a beginner along the transformative journey that is becoming a triathlete.

About the Author

Max Stoneking is a current Doctor of Physical Therapy Student and an avid triathlete. He started swimming at the age of 7 and continued with the sport into the college ranks before getting a start in triathlon. Along the way, he got to experience the training and competition at the highest level of swimming which served as a foundation for understanding what it means to develop as an athlete. Since starting in the sport of triathlon, he has taken home numerous top age group finishes and aspires to compete at a level on par with other elite amateurs. He has also taken on roles as an assistant swimming coach at Carroll University in Waukesha, Wisconsin, United States, and as an endurance coach for a small cohort of athletes in running and triathlon. Max is the epitome of a student of the sport and aims to relay that knowledge to athletes near and far. For more on Max, you can visit his Twitter profile @max_stoneking and his weekly Substack newsletter called Study + Sport: maxstoneking.substack.com.

HowExpert publishes how to guides on all topics from A to Z by everyday experts. Visit HowExpert.com to learn more.

About the Publisher

Byungjoon "BJ" Min is an author, publisher, entrepreneur, and the founder of HowExpert. He started off as a once broke convenience store clerk to eventually becoming a fulltime internet marketer and finding his niche in publishing. He is the founder and publisher of HowExpert where the mission is to discover, empower, and maximize everyday people's talents to ultimately make a positive impact in the world for all topics from A to Z. Visit BJMin.com and HowExpert.com to learn more. John 14:6

Recommended Resources

- HowExpert.com – How To Guides on All Topics from A to Z by Everyday Experts.
- HowExpert.com/free – Free HowExpert Email Newsletter.
- HowExpert.com/books – HowExpert Books
- HowExpert.com/courses – HowExpert Courses
- HowExpert.com/clothing – HowExpert Clothing
- HowExpert.com/membership – HowExpert Membership Site
- HowExpert.com/affiliates – HowExpert Affiliate Program
- HowExpert.com/jobs – HowExpert Jobs
- HowExpert.com/writers – Write About Your #1 Passion/Knowledge/Expertise & Become a HowExpert Author.
- HowExpert.com/resources – Additional HowExpert Recommended Resources
- YouTube.com/HowExpert – Subscribe to HowExpert YouTube.
- Instagram.com/HowExpert – Follow HowExpert on Instagram.
- Facebook.com/HowExpert – Follow HowExpert on Facebook.
- TikTok.com/@HowExpert – Follow HowExpert on TikTok.

Made in United States
Troutdale, OR
12/09/2024